POWERFUL PRESENTATIONS

Simple ideas for making a real impact

SECOND EDITION

JÖNS EHRENBORG and JOHN MATTOCK

KOGAN PAGE

First published in 1993

This edition 1997

The masculine pronoun has been used throughout this book. This stems from a desire to avoid ugly and cumbersome language, and no discrimination, prejudice or bias is intended.

Kogan Page Limited
120 Pentonville Road
London N1 9JN

© Jöns Ehrenborg and John Mattock, 1997

British Library Cataloguing in Publication Data

A CIP record for this book is available from the British Library.

ISBN 0 7494 2467 2

Typeset by Northern Phototypesetting Co. Ltd., Bolton

Printed in England by Clays Ltd, St Ives plc

Contents

Introduction

> If I want to succeed in guiding a human being towards a given goal, I must find him where he is, and start right there... To help a person, I must of course understand more than he does, but above all I must understand what he understands.
>
> *Søren Kierkegaard*

Most of this book is about *guiding human beings towards given goals*; it offers a set of tools for designing and delivering a persuasive presentation.

Many of the tools are thousands of years old: they were already in use when Kierkegaard took them up in the nineteenth century. Unfortunately the same tools are also in daily use by unscrupulous politicians and media charlatans. We can only hope you will put them to *good* use.

The book is for you if you sometimes feel that your presentations have gone stale, or if you doubt sometimes that your message has got through.

The chapters can be read in sequence, as a kind of seminar. We suggest you give a little time to reflection after each couple of pages, and have a go at the exercises.

Alternatively you can skim the book for half an hour to get the flavour, then put it on the shelf until you are preparing for your next presentation – at which point you take it down and dip into it a bit more deeply.

The picture we have in mind throughout the book – the reference point – is *you* delivering a fully prepared presentation, standing before a seated audience of a dozen or more, and equipped with the usual audio-visual equipment. (Yet this is not a book about body language, voice projection and flipchart technique; much of what we offer would be useful in a one-to-one encounter with your bank manager, or your teenage daughter.)

Following Kierkegaard's advice, we will begin with the human beings you are addressing in your presentation, and examine their state of mind as you stand up to speak.

1

What's going on in your listener's head?

A dialogue. He is talking to himself.

From the moment you begin your presentation, one part of your listener's mind is asking questions:

Is this message for me?

Can I believe this message?

Is the speaker on my side?

Another part* of his mind is hearing these questions, and trying to find the answers in what you are saying.

In this chapter we will take the three questions in turn, and show what you, the presenter, must do to make sure that your listener finds the right answers:

Yes, it's a good, useful message from somebody I can trust!

---

*Yet another part of his mind is wool-gathering – gazing out of the window, thinking about his love-life, worrying about his waistline. Later in the book we will suggest ways to make sure this doesn't happen *too* much – ways to grab his attention and keep it.

QUESTION ONE
IS THIS MESSAGE FOR ME?

Of course, your listener cannot answer this rationally, until he has listened to the whole of your message, right to the very end. But in fact, he is asking the question from the beginning.

This gives you a wonderful opportunity to get in quick with the right answer. You should *tell* your listener quite clearly:

Yes, this message *is* for you!

This is one of the most basic manipulations in advertising.

Many of the successful advertising campaigns are based on a deliberately naive premise: that the bank that gambles on the stock exchange with your money knows and cares about you personally, or that the company that makes catfood has a special interest in the welfare of your particular cat:

A higher rate deposit account, where your money will work harder for you!

Yummikins... because your cat deserves it!

The money, of course, is doing a lot of its work for the benefit of the bank. As for the cat, how can he 'deserve' anything when he never does anything for anybody else? Yet reason counts for little.

Much more important is *identification* – the process through which a listener says 'Ah! I am a shrewd investor and I own a lovely cat! These messages are aimed at me! I'll sit up and pay attention!' (Non-capitalist cat-haters who happen to be watching the TV just switch off mentally: 'This is nothing to do with me...')

The use of the word *YOU* in these commercial messages is vital. Look how much is lost if we drop the *YOU*: where money works harder!; because cats deserve it!

Consider

Your country needs you

versus

This country needs soldiers

or

Big Brother is watching you

versus

Big Brother is watching every citizen.

Mark Antony's great opening line (one of Shakespeare's Top Ten) achieves its result in a similarly direct way:

> Friends, Romans, countrymen, lend me your ears.

Antony is simply saying 'This message *is* for you, so listen!' (Much more about this piece of classical rhetoric later in the book.)

Not all advertising is so blatant in its use of *YOU*, *YOUR* and *YOURS*. Yet all successful advertising achieves this goal of identification somehow: the individual who is expected to remember and act on the message is made to feel that it is directed at him personally. In a typical TV spot the advertiser has 30 seconds to achieve this.

Exercise

Watch a battery of ads, on TV or at the cinema, and try to find the device in each ad. How does the advertiser involve the target audience?

(Often, it is by means of a joke. If a viewer, listener, reader smiles or laughs at an advertisement, the bond is very strong: 'This makes *me* laugh; it fits *my* sense of humour.' Less elegantly, a kind of moral blackmail takes place: '*Caring* mums use Frotho!')

The bond between the listeners and the message is made even stronger if the message is expressed in terms suited to the listener's world. Recruiting disciples among fishermen, Jesus Christ invited them:

> Come with me and I will make you fishers of men.

What this means to you

When you are convincing a dozen people, you have a great advantage over the creative department in an advertising agency. They have to make educated, highly expensive guesses at the inclinations of millions, and then aim messages at hundreds of thousands.

With a smaller, more focused target, you can shape your message to fit the occasion, and *tell your listeners that you are speaking to them*!

I believe this will be of special interest to all of you whose children have to cross this busy street

Have you noticed how young people these days never say 'Please' or 'Thank you'?

The advice I will offer is particularly aimed at anybody who hopes to pass this examination first time

Experiment

At a gathering of people (drinks party/coffee break at the conference/small talk around the lockers), position yourself at the opposite side of the room from somebody whose name you know – Peter Fletcher, let's say.

Start a conversation with somebody else, and insert PF's name into the conversation – in a normal tone of voice. Something like: 'Oh, if there's one person you should ask about roses, it's Peter Fletcher!', or 'I believe Peter Fletcher had a very similar experience when he sold his house recently.'

Nobody else in the room will pay any attention at all, but the chances are Peter Fletcher will stop what he is doing, look your way, smile, and mime 'talking about me?'

Warning

The most dangerous subject in the world is the subject where *you are a great expert or enthusiast*. You can so easily drone on about it, regardless of your audience, for your own interest or pleasure.

Your listener will sense this, and his internal dialogue will proceed like this:

Q: Is this message for me?

A: Obviously not. This bloke's talking to himself.

Quick tip

In the first couple of minutes, try to say *YOU / YOUR / YOURS* more than *ME / THEIR / OURS.*

QUESTION TWO
CAN I BELIEVE THIS MESSAGE?

When you meet a dog, and the dog sniffs your hand, he is making sure you are not a chicken, a lion, or another dog who is about to challenge him.

When you are setting out to present a case, you must let your audience sniff your hand – to make sure you are not a fanatic, a liar or a clown.

Your personal credibility depends on the plausibility of your message. Before you give your audience a new proposition to think about, you have to establish yourself as the source of good, true, wholesome ideas – or at least of accurate and useful information.

'At this point in the relationship, you have to provide us with a token of your sincerity,' Pogodin said...

The invitation dangled before Lewinter. He considered his laminated ID card, his MIT faculty card, his passport. But he knew that none of these would get him on the eight o'clock plane to Moscow.

'Look,' he said, 'I could give you the formula for the trajectory of one of the decoys in a MIRV. You can cable it to Moscow. Surely there must be somebody there who can vouch for its value.'

Without a flicker of expression, Pogodin offered the green notebook to Lewinter.

'Do you need a pen?' he asked politely.

Robert Littell,
The Defection of A J Lewinter

The best, truest, most wholesome ideas are the ones which your audience can check against what they already know or believe or feel. They hear what you say and hold it up against their own knowledge or opinions. If your first statement matches what they find in their own mental wardrobe, they will approve of it.

They won't object at all. They won't say 'What a waste of time to tell me something I already know!' Rather, they will smile and nod.

When you see that signal, your listener is telling you: 'I have checked this statement against what I know to be true; I find that it agrees; I am now prepared to believe the next thing you tell me.' Once they have started nodding, it will be easier to keep them nodding.

If you have established yourself already as a source of reliable facts and good ideas, the Green Channel will be open to you: you can deliver your key message direct into the audience's mind without too much scrutiny. It will be sympathetically received:

> He's right, you know. I had the same experience myself!

> How many times have I said the same thing?

> At last! Somebody to back up what I've been saying all these years!

> True, true. How very true!

Observation

When somebody recommends a book, a newspaper article, or a course of study, what is he more likely to say?

(a) This is really good; it reinforces a lot of things I believe in.

or

(b) This is really good; it forces me to admit I was wrong before.

When Mark Antony begins his great speech ('Friends, Romans, countrymen, lend me your ears') he has an immediate problem to solve: the Roman citizens in his audience know that he is a good friend to Julius Caesar, who has just been assassinated. They have been convinced by Brutus that Caesar was justly killed, and are in no mood now for a sentimental speech about what a great and good man he really was. Mark Antony knows (from years of rhetorical training) that he risks total rejection – *unless he assures his audience from the start that his message is a straight one.*

> I come to bury Caesar, not to praise him.

This really means: 'You all know I loved this man, and you are afraid that I will now try to manipulate you into loving him too. Don't worry, this is not that kind of speech! All I ask is a few moments of your time so we can get this unpleasant business out of the way.'

What this means to you

Before you try to influence your audience, win their trust. Give them a piece of information they already have; suggest an opinion they already hold; express an emotion they already feel.

The experienced persuader often goes one step further: he admits to one fact which obviously militates *against* his argument. Again, it will be a fact which is already familiar to the audience, or which they can deduce for themselves:

> Now you know from experience that a project like this entails an element of risk.

> One glance at the map will tell you that this route will take a little longer.

> I won't disguise it: finding and keeping the right staff will cost money.

In this way the speaker earns a *double* nod: *This person has told me something I already know, so I will nod in agreement; he has shown himself to be honest, astute and objective, so I will nod in approval.*

Notice also the careful phrasing in the three messages above. Each one implicitly flatters the audience: *You are clever people.*

These clever people, of course, want to be certain that you, as the speaker, are *competent* – in command of your material, and able to keep any promises you make. We return to the theme of competence in Chapter 5.

QUESTION THREE
IS THE SPEAKER ON MY SIDE?

We are not saying that the three questions occur in a given sequence. Provided you answer them all quickly and positively, you can handle them in any order.

Mark Antony chooses to answer our 'Question Three' before the other two:

> Friends, Romans, countrymen...

He could not possibly be more clear.

> Yes, I *am* on your side!

Similarly Queen Elizabeth I, speaking to her troops in the year of the Armada:

> I am come before you... being resolved in the midst and heat of the battle to live or die amongst you all – to lay down for my God and for my kingdom and for my people my honour and my blood, even in the dust...

And more economically, John F Kennedy:

> Ich bin ein Berliner.

Kennedy's audience of *real* Berliners, alone and frightened in a sea of Bolshevism, were very ready to believe they had an ally in the Oval Office.

Notice that these three expert speakers use simple, concrete language at these crucial moments. They are careful not to put up barriers by using fancy words or complex logic. Most audiences are immediately suspicious of smooth talkers with big vocabularies.

One of Shakespeare's most eloquent speakers is the Moor, Othello. When he is accused by her father of seducing Desdemona, he immediately promises to express his defence in simple terms:

Rude am I in my speech,
And little blest with the set phrase of peace...
I will a round unvarnished tale deliver...

In fact, Othello commands all the 'smooth parts of speech', and everybody at the Venetian court must have admired – perhaps even feared – his oratory. Yet when he makes a promise to be forthright in his dealing, his listeners settle themselves to a 'round unvarnished tale', reassured that they are in no danger of being manipulated.

A friend of ours recalls a visit to his school by a distinguished Old Boy – Field Marshal Lord Montgomery of Alamein. Monty had chosen to give out copies of his autobiography as prizes:

There are two kinds of book: good books and rotten books.
This is a good book. I wrote it.

Simple, clear schoolboy language, including the schoolboy term of disparagement: 'rotten'.

And every schoolboy in the audience had suffered plenty of rotten books. Here now was the big war hero admitting that he, too, had suffered!

Nineteen little words that had stuck in our friend's head for thirty years.

What this means to you

Tell your audience you are one of them, or at least that you can see things from their point of view.

Express yourself in simple terms, and show that you don't want to bamboozle everybody with words.

If possible, use a little of the audience's language to express a perception special to that audience.

Exercise

In each case, picture in your mind the speaker and the audience:

1. My grandfather, a carpenter, gave me a very important piece of advice…

2. When I was putting my time in on the assembly line at our factory down the road here…

3. I'm pleased to note that the apple pie in the refectory is still as substantial as when I was kicked out of the first eleven for missing training.

The one example that says it all

To revisit the first two lines from Mark Antony over Caesar's corpse:

> Friends, Romans, countrymen, lend me your ears.
> I come to bury Caesar, not to praise him.

In saying these words, Antony has encouraged his audience to believe: *An ally of mine wants to tell me something, and it will be simple, useful stuff.*

Throughout the speech that follows, he returns again and again to the themes:

❑ I am myself, and not playing any role

❑ I am a plain, blunt man

❑ I have no enemies; everybody trusts me

❑ I will put simple facts before you

❑ You know all this anyway

THE INTERNATIONAL ARENA

What these sections are for

At the end of each chapter or section, we shall consider what additional factors come into play when you, as speaker, are working across a culture gap.

We have studied at first hand, in many countries, the things that happen when communication 'goes international', and enjoyed the experience very much.

Academic models of cross-cultural transactions have been avoided, although we have certainly made use of them ourselves in interpreting what we see around us.

When we describe the sort of thing that happens, we will also try to offer practical advice on how to put it right.

Our general advice for those speaking to audiences across a culture gap, and hoping to make a good impression in the opening minutes, is:

Be clear

It is hard for an audience to be carried along by your message if they can't catch what you're saying. They will switch off at Question One: 'I don't know if this message is for me, because I can't really hear it.'

Example: When you first speak your name, or the name of your company or product, speak it loud and clear and slow to save embarrassment later. It is hard for a German ear to catch a Spanish sound, or for an American ear to take in a string of Hungarian.

Be attentive and sincere

Show that you want the listeners to get the message.

Example: If the local culture permits it, establish strong eye contact early on.

Be curious

Ask somebody who is experienced in the culture what you should expect from the audience.

Examples: Will they be happy to engage in argument (like the Dutch, we find), or will they tend to be passive and wait for you to deliver all the ideas (like some Asian cultures)? Do they appreciate direct sincerity (like most Slavs), or a layer of irony (like the English)?

Be flexible

Don't let your stereotypes take over. The generalizations in the paragraph above are out of date.

Examples: As you read this, many young Chinese and Indonesian managers are developing a more open, combative style – so you can expect more interaction during your presentation in Shanghai. And the spirit of political correctness is leading more and more English people to abandon irony and most other forms of humour – so be careful of seeming cynical to a group of sincere health workers in North Cheshire.

Monitor the feedback carefully

The signals you are getting from your audience might not mean what you think.

Examples: The popular one is of the Japanese nodding and saying, 'Yes… yes… yes…' – not to mean 'I agree', or even 'I understand' but only 'I am paying attention'. A version closer to us is of an American who went to live in Zurich, and felt uncomfortable at all the 'Ja… ja…' noises he heard when he was speaking to people. They were saying: 'Go on, I'm listening', but the man from Pittsburgh was receiving a different message: 'Yah, yah… yah, yah… I'm bored, and I don't really believe you.'

Be yourself

Indicate that you know something of the culture you are speaking to, but stay rooted in what you are.

Example: Some Westerners visiting countries in the old Soviet bloc have left their smartest clothes at home in Bonn or Paris, for fear of seeming to flaunt their wealth. In fact, Russian and Hungarian audiences have a positive attitude to good clothes: 'This person is clearly onto something good. I will listen…'

Cross-cultural example from the preceding question:

We discussed the power of the word *YOU* in advertising. In some cultures, people resent being 'softened up' in this way.

A European is happy to hear a speaker say 'There are some aspects of this product which will certainly appeal to you.' He recognizes, and dislikes, the Americanness of such messages as: 'We're sincerely proud to bring to you personally the dishwasher of your dreams!'

Conversely, Americans are sometimes confused by the more laconic European style – especially by British understatement. Many an American has said, after a sales presentation by an Englishman: 'Interesting talk, but I don't feel he really *believes* in the product. He just didn't seem to care.'

There is a fine borderline between 'selling the benefits' and 'irritating presumption', and different cultures draw the line in different places.

2

What will stick in your listener's memory?

In all walks of business, useful ideas *on paper* are used more for later reference than for immediate communication. Skim it, put it on the shelf, go back to it later.

Written information should be *easy to find again*.

The report you write for the board, or the catalogue you lay out for your customers, must have a structure that helps them to locate an idea or a product quickly the next time they need it.

Structure is also important in a spoken communication, as we shall see later, but only because a clear structure helps the audience to follow what you say, and store the information (or argument) in their minds.

Live communication should be *easy to remember*.

Much research has gone into the workings of the human memory. To simplify things grossly, we have a brain divided into two halves, and the two halves are good at different things.

LEFT BRAIN = LOGICAL + QUICKLY LOST

RIGHT BRAIN = ROMANTIC + EASILY REMEMBERED

People remember items much more easily if the items are connected to right brain stimulation – along with music, art, sensory activity and emotion. Consider how much small children learn from singing songs, looking at pictures, playing with toys and giving and receiving love.

Some speakers – failed politicians, bad teachers, starving salesmen – choose to suppose that their audiences will remember the words they speak without additional help. Hopeless: ordinary Language goes on in the Left brain, and is soon forgotten – driven out by the next stream of words.

Some presenters these days try to make an impression by throwing up screen after screen of lists, tables and bullet points. Not much better. Bullet points lost all their impact a long time ago. These so-called 'visual aids' are just lists of words to help the speaker remember what he wants to say next, and so of virtually no interest to the audience.

We have been present at conferences where the audience has groaned out loud as the fifth speaker of the day has started spraying bullet points around the room. The projector – 35mm, or overhead, or videobeam – should be used to *stimulate the right brain*, by showing

pictures!

Your right-brain memory is very effective. It works by taking a piece of information and 'hooking' it to other things already in the memory. The visual hook is the strongest and sharpest – particularly if the picture is of a person (you the presenter, for example).

Exercise

Cast your mind back to a speech or lecture or presentation you have sat through. (It really doesn't matter how long ago it was.) How much can you recall? How many numbers? Dates? Names? Can you actually bring back to mind the words the speaker used?

Now some rather different questions to answer from memory: Was the speaker a man or a woman? Attractive? What colour hair? Standing or sitting? A lot of arm-waving or a static performance? Formal or relaxed? Happy or sad?

What this means to you

Think of yourself as a visual aid. Carry yourself well, look happy, be open and human. (But don't be so flamboyant that the audience remembers you and not the message.)

Move about the stage area – your working space – to vary the stimulus; change the frame in your viewer's mind, like a new camera angle. (But don't run around like a rat in its cage.)

When you are ready to deliver your key message in a few well-chosen words, clear the podium for a minute – switch off the projector and clean the whiteboard. Let the audience concentrate on you personally.

You will provide a strong visual hook for your audience's right-brain memory to attach to.

People remember visual stimuli

Millions of adults still know that Tintin has a funny haircut and Captain Haddock goes red in the face when he drinks.

Many medieval monks underwent intensive training, using a range of techniques and tools, so that they could commit long religious texts to memory. A Bible was too precious (and heavy) to carry on difficult journeys. The documents the monks studied were beautifully illuminated – headers and margins of plants and animals, angels and devils, Noah and his sons. These images had a serious purpose – to provide memory hooks and so help the text stick in the mind of the reader.

To take an example nearer the present, can you remember either of the names of the authors of this book? We don't flatter ourselves.

But do you remember the colours on the cover of the book?

Sometimes you want the audience to remember a few key words. It is perfectly all right to put them up on the screen in big letters:

PROFITABILITY

GROWTH

ZERO-DEFECT

COMMUNICATION

But *don't expect them to remember all four words an hour later*. You will improve the score greatly if you attach an *icon* to each word.

One or two simple things from your PC can help.

PROFITABILITY
£$

GROWTH
↗

ZERO-DEFECT
OK

COMMUNICATION
" "

You can be much more creative with two or three coloured markers and a sheet of paper. (Trace it onto acetate for the OHP, or scan it into your PC for projection through the videobeam.)

Simple, tidy, hand-drawn visuals can be very warm and memorable. There are some scattered around this chapter.

People remember analogies and symbols

The icons above (£$ = profitability, } " " = communication, etc) are neat enough, but they are not as strong as when a powerful argument is attached.

The Hammer and Sickle is quick and easy to recognize, even when daubed on a wall, and it delivers a message about the union of proles and peasants. The Yin-Yang symbol contains a whole story of opposing forces in a balanced universe. The big red heart for 'I love New York' brought a considerable change in the life of the city.

An early example is the Shamrock – the little plant with the trefoil leaf, which is now the Irish national emblem, and the logo of Aer Lingus. Tradition has it that Saint Patrick used it 1500 years ago as a way of explaining to simple peasants the rather complex doctrine of the Holy Trinity. He used it as a prop or mnemonic device. As a *visual aid*. Those who heard Patrick use the analogy would be reminded of it every time they saw a patch of shamrock growing.

Once your words leave your lips, they are out of your control. Speaking a sentence to an audience is like throwing a rock into a pond: the splash is heard and felt, and the ripples spread, bobbing leaves and twigs about, bending the plants at the rim, stirring up the mud on the bottom. Your words set off chain reactions – unconscious connotations and personal associations – in your listeners' minds. Your meaning is soon distorted or lost. (This effect is well-recognized, and the basis of many parlour pastimes and TV game shows.)

Saint Patrick knew that people remember what they have seen with their eyes and in their minds – *not* the words they have heard.

One sure way to make a moment more memorable is to attract and surprise the eyes of your audience.

WHAT IS *NOT* A VISUAL AID?

A table of production output estimates, photographed onto a 35mm slide from a company report, is not a visual aid. A system diagram of a telephone exchange, with code numbers and acronyms, is not a visual aid – especially if it has the speaker's e-mail address in tiny print at the bottom. The first three paragraphs of the CEO's latest inspirational speech do not make a visual aid, even with a photograph of the great man displayed alongside.

90 per cent of what is shown to audiences during business presentations is a waste of effort at best. Often it is so bad it diminishes the speaker in the minds of the audience: 'This speaker has no discernment.' At worst, the badly designed material on the screen sends out an implicit insult: 'I care so little about you as an audience that I can't be bothered to produce something decent for you to look at.'

If your visual aid does not help the audience to understand and remember the point which you are making, then

Replace it or leave it out.

The things people say

'I know you can't actually see the figures on this slide; I had a lot of detail to squeeze in. I'll read it out to you.'

'My son always jokes when he sees me packing for a business trip: "Good old Dad – 100 OPM –" He means Overheads Per Minute.'

'I found this cartoon in a magazine I was reading. It hasn't really got a lot to do with my theme today, which as you will remember is "leadership", but I found it amusing.'

'Why not bung another graph in, it can't do any harm.'

What this means to you

During your presentation, the visual channel into your audience's mind is the most immediately powerful. Well used, it will help you immensely.

But a bad visual, or a visual badly used, or *too many* visuals, will do serious damage to your image as a presenter – offering a lasting picture of you performing badly.

WHAT IS *ALMOST* A VISUAL AID?

The people who make personal computers and graphic software packages want you to buy their products. They say to you:

- ❏ Look at these *graphs! pie charts! histograms!* In millions of colours!
- ❏ Aren't they *professional! impressive! expensive-looking*!
- ❏ Now your customer will *buy your products*! The board will *accept your proposal*! Your boss will *give you a pay-rise*!

We have grave doubts about all this. We are afraid that often the audience is thinking:

- ❏ Look! They're *all the same*!
- ❏ Aren't they *dull*!
- ❏ Now we know that you can work a PC mouse *Big deal*!

We accept that charts, diagrams and similar devices can be helpful when you are *explaining* a point, but they do not stimulate the imagination, nor lodge themselves in the memory.

If you are using 'presentations software'

If you follow the guidelines and models that come with the package, your visual aids will contain more verbal than visual information. If you really insist on putting up screens full of words (in spite of everything we have said so far), then *keep it simple*.

- ❏ Only use 2 different fonts, in 2 different point sizes
- ❏ Don't go crazy with *italics*, CAPITALS *and* **BOLD**
- ❏ Don't use fancy borders which are more interesting than the words inside them

This last habit is an example of *decoration*, and it serves no real purpose. Many presentation programs contain lots of pictures for you to *decorate* your presentation with – little cartoon executives planting flags on mountains (EXCELLENCE) or switched-on light-bulbs (GOOD IDEA!). Unfortunately, many of your audience have also bought such programs and, like you, they have browsed through the pictures available. So when you click your radio mouse and the picture comes up, they stop concentrating on what you are saying and instead start thinking: 'I wonder what software he's using...' – or even 'He's a bit out-of-date; that picture's from an old version of the software.'

Much better to find ways of using the software creatively, to produce fresh-looking visual aids to support your main ideas.

The following six diagrams are a sequence of overheads produced on a basic PC graphics package, very simply and quickly.

1. The theme: Antenna ABC fixed in the mind as a simple shape;
2. The three advantages of Antenna ABC, each with a visual 'hook';
3. Revenue advantages explained in more detail;
4. Capacity advantages explained in more detail;
5. Freedom advantages explained in more detail;
6. Summary: the three great advantages of Antenna ABC.

One final point about digitalized presentations: we mentioned earlier the importance of *clearing the podium* to permit you to talk directly and sincerely to your audience. With computer-generated visuals now in common use, we have noticed a much increased tendency for the visuals to take over the show. With many programmes, it is difficult to switch off the beam once the presentation has started; if yours has this defect, then insert a 'visual' of a blank square – dark blue or green – after each real visual. Then you can switch immediately to a non-distracting background if, for example, you have to handle an unexpected question from the audience.

What this means to you

Ask yourself sincerely: Do you want the main ideas in your presentation to be remembered? If the answer is no, then illustrate it in the same style as all the other ideas in all the other presentations your audience is watching these days. Use the computer graphics package, with standard layouts. Then you will be one of the crowd.

```
O     O     O     O     O     O     O     O
+     +     +     +     +     +     +     +
^     ^     ^     ^     ^     ^     ^     ^
```

Alternatively, you could be audacious! Decide to be memorable! Turn the clock back! Be primitive! *Make your own visual in your own style!*

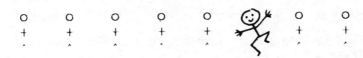

HOW TO MAKE A *GOOD* VISUAL AID

Accept that your first idea will not be your best

No artist can say: 'I will consult my muse over coffee at eleven o'clock, and start painting at ten past.' Why should you be different?

When you are translating from the world of words and concepts to the world of visual representation, you should be prepared to discard your first few efforts.

Even if all you want is a functional, attractive diagram to support a common-sense argument, you are setting out on a creative journey.

Give the creative process a chance

Jot a few ideas down in pencil on an ordinary notepad. Put them aside and do something else for a while. Jot a few new ideas down with fat felt-tips on a white board. Set them aside and go for lunch. Modify your earlier ideas using different coloured pens and paper. Go home and sleep on it. The quiet periods are known variously as 'getting some distance', 'referring the matter to your subconscious' or 'incubating'.

The changes in colour and medium are a good way to lighten up and stimulate the right brain – where all the visualizing takes place.

Three creative ten-minute sessions, with your right brain running free, will produce more fresh ideas than a solid two hours stuck in a rut in the left brain.

Use another person to get your creative juices running

Sit down with a friend over a beer, and talk it through – making sure you have a ball-point pen and plenty of beermats to draw on. One of the beermats might easily become the heart of the company's next million-dollar advertising campaign.

Simplify, simplify, simplify

Your key drawing or diagram must be designed as an aid to memory. If there is too much detail, the minds of your audience will flush away all the peripheral information, and with it your central point:

> **You give me too much to remember,**
> **so I will remember nothing.**

Check that the picture means what you want it to mean

Choose a friend or colleague who knows little about the message you are trying to transmit. Show him the draft of your visual with very little comment – just enough context so he can try to grasp the meaning of your picture. Then ask him to talk about what he sees and how he interprets it. Listen carefully.

If your visual aid is transmitting the wrong message, or is ambiguous or impenetrable, don't try to defend or justify it. Take it away and modify it. Perhaps better, take it away and scrap it.

Keep revising your draft

If the idea seems to work, then play around with it. You are working with several key variables:

COLOUR

SHAPE

POSITION

SIZE

(Choose a blue crayon from the box; decide to draw a hippopotamus; in the top right-hand corner of the paper; a little fat one.)

Spread the various versions out on your sitting room floor and look objectively. Invite opinions from colleagues.

One version of your picture will seem stronger and clearer than the others. Select that one for final production. (If you then pass it on to your company's drawing office, or graphics department, insist that they produce the piece according to your specifications, and do not 'improve' things when your back is turned.

Check that the final version is easy to see

If you are going to use an OHP transparency, you should be able to prop the acetate on a shelf, against a white wall, and read it from four paces away. If it is too small to pass that test, when you project it on the screen, the people in the back row of the auditorium will suffer eye strain and irritation.

Even better, ask a colleague to read it on the shelf. Since you already know what it says, you could optimistically convince yourself that it is legible over any distance.

For printed words we recommend 36-point for headings and 28-point for the rest.

As for colour, high contrast is best – black or dark blue on white or yellow; white or yellow reversed out of black or dark blue. Red is dramatic at close range, on the printed page, but it is less striking at a distance.

Colour rules in heraldry

In the Middle Ages, a knight in full armour, visor and all, was unrecognizable to friend or enemy. So he wore a surcoat and bore a shield, with his armorial bearings – his coat of arms.

It was vital that the markings should be discernible at a great distance; longbows were powerful and accurate.

The rules of heraldry show that its practitioners had a good understanding of how the human eye works – especially seeing things clearly at a distance. The principle they applied was *maximum contrast*.

There are five principal colours in heraldry: red, blue, black, green and purple. There are two metals: gold (yellow) and silver (white). On a metal background, only a colour could be used. On a coloured ground, only a metal. Never metal on metal, nor colour on colour.

If you have a PC and a colour printer, you will be tempted to play around with the colour palette in your software. If you are drawing something like this:

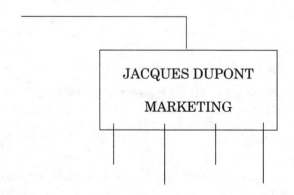

you should never fill the box with red, and print poor M. Dupont's name in purple. He would be virtually invisible.

Translating words into simple drawings

'When I first joined the department, I found an atmosphere of mistrust and recrimination':

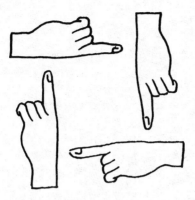

'If we are to survive, we must support each other as a team':

Translating numbers into diagrams

'20 per cent of the people in the world consume 80 per cent of the world's resources':

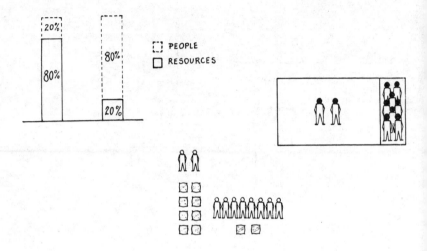

All these diagrams illustrate the same point. Which works best for you? Finally, it's subjective. Once more, check with other people to make sure the meaning is clear. *Not* like this:

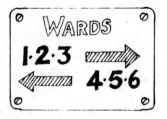

Make the image simple. Not like this:

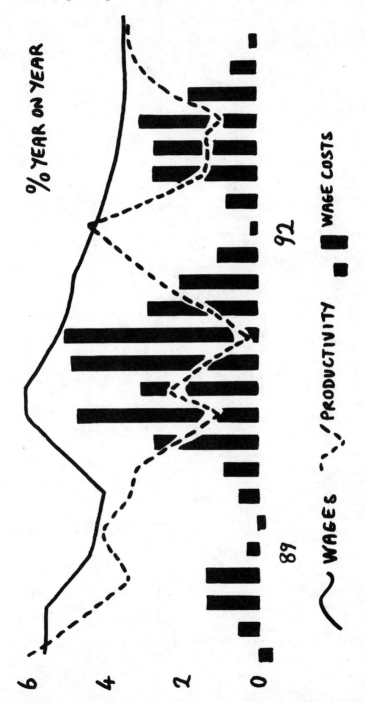

This is clear and simple:

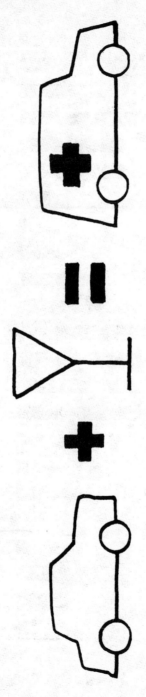

It is also stimulating, because it *engages* the viewer, forcing the audience to play a little arithmetic game in their heads.

Audiences love it if you leave a little work for their brains to do. This is Picasso's sketch of Don Quixote and Sancho Panza. Look how rudimentary the sun is, and the central windmill.

Now look more closely at Sancho Panza's donkey. Only three legs. Picasso gives you enough information to be sure it is a donkey (standing-up-animal-with-long-ears), and leaves you to fill in the details just below the level of consciousness.

What this means to you

Make sure your visual aids are

CLEAR

EASY TO SEE, EASY TO GRASP

SIMPLE

NO DECORATION OR CLUTTER

STIMULATING

LEAVING SOMETHING FOR THE AUDIENCE TO DO

HOW TO MAKE YOUR PICTURE SUPPORT YOUR MESSAGE

Start with a clear message

It is very hard to draw a clear picture of a garbled idea.

Put another way: if your idea cannot be represented in a clear and simple picture, it might just be a woolly and undisciplined idea.

Or put yet another way: good clear ideas translate easily into strong memorable images.

The acid test of many a management idea has occurred at the meeting called to discuss the question: 'How do we communicate this?'

Accept that it won't be easy

The professional propagandists and advertising experts charge high fees with good reason. It is brain-aching work to produce a memorable picture of your idea, but it is a skill for which you can train.

Exercise

Make a rough sketch to illustrate each of these ideas:
- ❏ Keeping fit can be terribly boring
- ❏ Always telephone your mother on her birthday
- ❏ A penny saved is a penny earned
- ❏ Our department is overworked and short of resources
- ❏ Our customers are eagerly awaiting the new product

Use strong images only in support of your important points

If by now you appreciate the power of images to *reinforce* your main message, you will also accept a warning about the power of images to *undermine* the message, or *distract* the audience's attention.

Suppose that you have three key points to make during your presentation. Points one and two you deliver with no support from visual aids. Then, with point three, you produce a striking, well-made picture. Your audience will certainly remember the final point much more clearly than the other two.

An even worse mistake is to show a graph of your discounted cash flow forecast, and follow it immediately with a colour photograph of a Pacific beach at sunset.

Be proud of the visual you have made

Many people, perhaps the victims of heavy-handed teaching methods during childhood, are reluctant to display 'artistic' work in public. On the presentation platform this often comes out as a feeble apology to the audience: 'I'm afraid this isn't really a proper slide. I made it myself.'

If you have worked creatively, been critical of your own first efforts, and audience-tested the visual aid in advance, then it is wrong to be diffident or apologetic. Say:

I think this picture sums it up for me, and I invite you to consider it for a moment.

Or:

There is one image I would like you to take away with you today, and here it is.

Illustrative anecdote

A cocktail party was given at the offices of *New Yorker* magazine, and the senior editor met one of the cartoonists for the first time.

Editor: I looked closely at the last cartoon you did for us: there were only eight strokes of the pen in it. And we paid you three thousand dollars.

Cartoonist: If I could have made the same joke with just seven penstrokes, I would have charged you *five* thousand dollars.

What this means to you

Ask yourself:

In one short sentence, what do I want my audience to take away with them from my presentation?
Then do everything you can to make a simple picture of that idea. If you succeed, the clarity of the picture will feed back into the power of the words you choose, your confidence will grow, and the picture itself will lodge in your audience's memory.

You will make a much greater impact.

HOW TO *HANDLE* YOUR VISUAL AIDS

Trim the dead wood

What do you sense when you are sitting in the audience and a presenter mounts the stage with both hands full of OHP slides?

Pleasurable anticipation? A thrill of excitement, perhaps? Or a sinking feeling and an inward groan: 'Here comes another human stroboscope.'

When you are packing for a trip, it is natural to take a few things along 'just in case' – like handfuls of 'potentially useful' slides.

When you arrive in your hotel and before the conference begins, take the 20 slides you packed for the trip, and spread them on the floor of your room. Sort them into three piles:

NEED TO SHOW	NICE TO SHOW (MAYBE)	NO WAY
2	4	14

Take the first pile to the platform in your hand. Have the second in your briefcase: some of them might come in useful during the Question-and-Answer session. Bury the third pile under the dirty laundry in your suitcase.

Make a final check of legibility

If at all possible, test your visual in the real situation. Throw it on the screen and go up into the back corner of the room, and be honest: Can everybody really see it?

If there are awkward corners, you might be able to keep people out of them.

Avoid gadgetry

There are a lot of conference hotels and company training centres with:

❑ radio microphones (clonk-hiss-silence);

❑ laser pointers (tremble-wobble-jerk);

❑ remote control video consoles ('No, that's the Fast Forward, not the Pause'); and

❑ enthusiastic technical assistants who want to persuade you to try them.

Smile politely, and refuse. A white-board and/or a flipchart, and a way of projecting images, is all you need.

Let your visuals speak

... which is a polite way of saying

Shut up while I'm looking at the nice picture

When your graphic goes up on the screen, or you reveal the next page of the flip chart, or unveil the scale model of the new yachting marina, step away and look quietly towards your audience. They will study the new information until they are comfortable with it – until they are ready for you to start giving a commentary on the picture. When they are ready for that, they will look towards you. When most of them are looking towards you, begin speaking.

This is difficult to do, because it seems like a terribly long time – but only to you as the presenter, because your adrenaline is high and your whole system is in a great hurry.

What this means to you

You are in control – not the equipment, not the visuals.

If you want the audience to have confidence in you, make it clear that you are in control.

THE INTERNATIONAL ARENA: PICTURES

We all adjust the way we explain a thing, or persuade a person, according to the age and experience of our listener. We speak in different ways to our bank managers and our teenage daughters.

Yet in the days of global business, it is very easy to stand before an audience of grey suits or golf sweaters in an air-conditioned conference suite *and forget they are from very different backgrounds*.

Don't worry too much

There is a set of behaviours proper to the international business community – the 'Hilton Culture', the Frequent Flyers.

It is fairly easy to Mind Your Manners in these circles, provided you behave in a gentle, moderately formal way. Be polite and speak clearly, and your audience of 'foreigners' will be at ease.

Nonetheless, it is important to adapt yourself to local sensitivities, in order to show that you care. When a Japanese man gives you his business card, treat it with great respect. At dinner in Switzerland, it is pleasant for everybody if you know how to handle your wine glass.

And your presentation will be more attractive to a Muslim audience if you avoid unnecessary stress on deadlines and timetables.

Denotation (a fancy word for 'meaning')

When you are using a visual to carry your message make sure it means the same when it arrives at the receiver as when it left the transmitter.

Some cultures read from right to left, so the message advertising ACME indigestion pills didn't travel very well:

An English schoolboy would be satisfied with these marks on his arithmetic homework:

But in Sweden the meaning of ticks and crosses is reversed.

INSTALLATION TIME MAINTENANCE COST RANGE OF APPLICATIONS

This picture carries the wrong message: 'Our equipment takes time to install and is costly to maintain. And it isn't very much use to you.'

What this means to you

Check your visual aid with a national of the culture you are going to address, asking:

Has this any meaning? If so, what?

If something is wrong, work with a national to find an alternative visual which *does* deliver your message. If you can't find such an

---

Connotations and Associations (what it reminds you of)

The computer company's sales department produced a slide with a cartoon showing a lion-tamer, in the centre of the circus ring with his whip and revolver, and a number of well-disciplined lions disposed about the ring on little platforms. The idea was that the main computer program (lion tamer) had the subsidiary routines (lions) well under control.

The visual was a disaster in a presentation to the civil service procurement department in a certain African country. For them, the lions were the spirit of the nation, subdued by a white man in the uniform of a colonial army.

In Western Europe or North America, if you draw a mouse badly, you can make it look more like a mouse by putting a piece of cheese in the picture – and you make it look like cheese by drawing big holes in it.

In many parts of the world, cheese is soft runny stuff quite without holes. And mice have only been known to eat grain.

The piggy bank is a symbol for money, savings and general prudence in the West. The convention is not recognized in countries where the pig is reviled as unclean.

Again we say: *check with a local.*

Dictionaries of Symbols exist covering many cultures, but usually they only define or explain the *denotations* of any given symbol. So the treatment of the Swastika, a very ancient symbol with great religious significance, might mention Nazism only in the last paragraph. The enormous *connotations* and *associations* of such symbols are often difficult to pin down academically.

One good way to tune in to the iconography of a culture which is new to you is to spend a little time watching the local TV commercials, or flicking through newspapers and magazines.

3

What else will reach your listener's mind and heart?

STORIES AND EMOTIONS

We can experience discomfort at a screen adaptation of a story we already know: 'I don't think the dungeon scene was gloomy enough'; 'I've always seen Mr Pickwick as much fatter than that'; 'She's not at all my idea of a Fairy Godmother!'

We have a special relationship with the pictures in our minds.

To put a picture of Michael Jackson into the mind of your listener, you do not have to *show* him a picture. You just have to say 'Michael Jackson', and he will immediately get a mental image.

The mental image will not be a complete picture. Perhaps just the lock of hair, a dance step or one glittering glove.

It will be your listener's own picture. This is often more useful to you, the presenter, than forcing your own picture upon him.

A famous 1960s radio advertisement

Advertising on radio is primitive, you say? It has no visual impact? OK, one commercial coming up!

First we empty Lake Superior. (Sound effect of bath draining)

Next, we refill it with chocolate malted milk.

And using every hose from the New York City Fire Department, we spray a fifty-foot layer of whipped cream on top. (Fire engine sound effects)

And now, a five-ton maraschino cherry, dropped from a height of 30,000 feet. Cue the US air force. (Droning big bombers... SPLOSH!)

OK. Let's see you do that on TV!

Here is Mark Antony again, putting a picture in the minds of his listeners:

> If you have tears, prepare to shed them now.
> You all do know this mantle. I remember
> The first time ever Caesar put it on.
> 'Twas on a summer's evening in his tent,
> That day he overcame the Nervii.

The ability to conjure up pictures in the mind when stimulated by a word, we can call *visualisation*. Some people are better at it than others, but every human being has the power to some degree.

For example, we find that engineering types, and particularly software writers, are often reluctant at first to play games in the right brain. Yet if they are in your audience, they also will be forced to visualize – and therefore remember better – if you tell them a story.

When we listen to a story – an anecdote, a tale or a saga – we visualize scenes in our minds, step by step, to help us follow the story. Radio producers call it 'The Theatre of the Mind'.

The trick of visualization is the reason why stories are such a vigorous element in every culture: visualization is fun.

You probably have stronger memories of stories you heard as a child, all those years ago, than you have of many recent presentations which had no story.

Stories play a vital rule in the memory of a tribe. Before the days of writing, stories were used to pass on laws and codes of ethics, and a sense of tribal identity. The tales of Beowulf, King Arthur and the Thief of Baghdad were not originally made for the entertainment of children.

HOW TO TELL A USEFUL STORY

'How to Tell a Great Story', in the bar-room sense of 'Harry tells really great stories', is the subject of a different book. And many books have been written about the story-telling skills of Guy de Maupassant or Herman Melville.

This book is about making presentations, so we define 'useful' here as 'helpful to your audience in remembering your important points'.

To help your audience remember, your story must come across well. There are techniques to be borrowed.

Make your stories close to your listener's experiences

If you are addressing an audience of trade unionists in the North of England, they will not warm to a story set in a gay disco in Sydney.

Yet if you are speaking to an audience of young mothers, they will create vivid detail in their minds to support a story set in a maternity hospital.

Children will not really absorb tales of *crime passionnel*, but farmers will empathize with stories about hard winters.

Shepherds, merchants, fishermen and soldiers in ancient Judaea wanted simple, memorable stories about people in their situation. So Jesus Christ, in his parables, gave them precisely that.

Borrow a technique from Christ's parables

Put people at the centre of your story

Or even better, one central person. Like the hero in a novel.

We have been given wonderful insights into whole social systems by authors who describe the adventures of one character – *Tom Jones*, *Candide*, Bazarov in *Fathers and Sons*.

So don't just say, 'There are difficulties for passengers transferring flights at busy airports in peak periods.' Say rather, 'There was a chap once travelling – or at least trying to travel – from Milan to Toronto via London.'

Borrow a tool from the novelists

Give names to your characters

Cast your mind back to your childhood reading, or video viewing. How many names of characters can you remember? The list is surprisingly long. (We've already mentioned Tintin and Captain Haddock.)

In some cases you can perhaps remember the name of a character more readily than the story – or you have the story filed in your mind under the name of the character. What would the chocolate factory be without Willy Wonka? The story of Hansel and Gretel is absolutely their story. Long John Silver is not just any old sailor with a parrot and a wooden leg.

Don't just say, 'A colleague of mine had an interesting experience a couple of weeks ago. He was travelling...' Say instead, 'I have a colleague called Joe Kelly. Some of you know him – big guy, golf crazy. Anyway, Joe Kelly was travelling...'

Borrow a trick from children's writers

Give your story a clear moral

Your story should have a point to it. Remember: just like a strong picture on the screen, the story will live in your audience's memory, so it should be connected with your message, shouldn't it?

We can reconstruct the message 'slow and steady wins the race', from the fable of the hare and the tortoise, by Aesop.

When we read La Fontaine's fable of the fox, the crow and the cheese, we receive a warning about the dangers of vanity.

When you finish your story, you can say: 'The moral (or point, or message) of this story is...' and then reinforce your point.

Borrow something from the fabulists

Let your audience do some of the work

'An Englishman, an Irishman and a Scotsman were waiting for the ferry...' The bar-room story-teller does not tell us which tartan the Scotsman's kilt was made of. His listeners do not ask what time the ferry is due.

Leave out unnecessary detail and permit the imagination of each individual in your audience to supply the little touches of colour.

Borrow from the bar-stool joker

Deliver the story with punch

Many languages make use of what is called 'the dramatic present' – 'So there I am, standing on the corner outside the betting shop, and this bloke with a bowler hat comes up to me, and he says... ' The use of the present tense – *am*, *comes*, *says* – gives a sense of immediate excitement.

Stand-up comics frequently deliver their material in the dramatic present.

Your audience will feel an enlivening change of tempo if you do the same.

Borrow a bit of style from the stand-up comic

What this means to you

Recognize the power of your audience's imagination, and let it work for you.

Be economical. Give the audience a frame to work in, and leave them to put the picture in the frame.

The lazy father's way to tell a bedtime story

Father: OK, John Christopher, just one story before you go to sleep. Now, shall we have a mountain, a forest or a river?

Child: Forest!

F: Forest it is. Think about it for a moment, because I'll

	ask you to tell me in a minute what it's like. Now, do we need a witch, a rabbit, or a Royal Canadian Mounted Policeman?
C:	Mountie!
F:	What's his name?
C:	Wizwoz!
F:	OK. Wizwoz the Mountie rode into the forest. What did you say it was like?
C:	All dark and wet and slimy with things in it.
F:	We'll come back to the things later. First, we have to establish why Wizwoz was going into the dark, wet, slimy forest...
C:	Because that's where the dentist lived, and Wizwoz had toothache.

To be continued...

So *visuals* are easy to remember, and *stories* are a good way of appealing to the visual part of the audience's mind. Anything else?

Yes, sorry to say it, but your audience would love to see you displaying some *emotion*.

USING EMOTION TO GOOD EFFECT

Be professional

There is an strong element of repression in many workplaces: if everybody is to get along together and produce results, then we can't afford to let emotions rip in the office.

Our systems of appraisal and reward tend to encourage bland, dispassionate behaviour. There is a negative term for the opposite: 'abrasive'.

So many people spend their careers thinking that to be *emotionally involved* with a piece of work is to be *unprofessional*. Displays of emotion have no place in the bank manager's office, the doctor's surgery, the academic tutor's study.

Expert, mature communicators, however, step through such inhibitions, and gain power by reintroducing emotion to the workplace.

How would you feel if your bank manager said, 'I've given a lot of thought to your case, and it would give me a great deal of pleasure to see your new business flourishing'?

Or the doctor: 'I've known you a long time now, and I really care about your welfare. I hate to see you damaging yourself with all this terrible rubbish you eat and drink'?

Or the tutor: 'Let's stop mincing words, shall we? The reason you have been performing badly this year is that you are on the wrong course. It upsets me personally to say so because, as you know, I love the subject, but...'?

Are these unprofessional statements? Only if they are insincere or backed by insufficient consideration If emotion is appropriate to the subject it is a very powerful communications tool.

> There was no denying the fact that words spoken from a full heart carry more weight than all the artifices of rhetoric.
>
> C S Forester, *A Ship of the Line*

We see a spectrum or scale:

INFORM ....**PERSUADE**

Each presentation you make, or each section in each presentation, is positioned somewhere along this scale.

Towards the 'inform' end, when you are explaining how to read a gas meter, or the purpose of discounted cash flow forecasting, there is no place for passion.

The more you move towards 'persuade', the more free you are to show strong personal feelings.

Exercise moderation

Hitler often appeared to lose control of his emotions. The power of his oratory sprang largely from this effect. Certainly his audiences perceived his rantings as totally sincere.

Trained actors are good at pretending to feel emotions. Yet Othello often smiles at the curtain call, minutes after killing Desdemona and himself in an uncontrollable fit of jealous rage.

As a professional presenter, you should neither lose control, nor let the audience feel you are just putting on an act. But you *should* let your feelings show, in a direct and unaffected way, at crucial moments. The audience is very quick to read your feelings, and if the only thing you are feeling is boredom, they will see it and be infected by it. Conversely, a little genuine enthusiasm is very infectious.

Don't pretend

'We are pleased to welcome as our after-dinner speaker Sir Henry Trumpington, who has just returned from his epic trip by canoe and hang-glider from Alaska to Cape Horn. His presence among us is very fitting, I think – for I have often said that our profession of accountancy is a great and exciting adventure.'

False heartiness, cheap sincerity, crocodile tears – all to be avoided.

Practise the emotional moments

When you deliver the good news, will you show how happy you are with a quiet smile, or by opening your arms wide and gazing heavenwards?

When you break the bad news, with furrowed brow, will you send your audience into a hopeless depression, or will you give them determination to work hard and improve the situation?

Can you talk about your own greatest hope for the future with controlled passion?

Help your audience to share the emotion

Mark Antony, in his great oration, teases his audience: has Caesar left the people something in his will?

>   which, pardon me, I do not mean to read...
>   It will inflame you, it will make you mad.

Antony is connecting two emotions in the audience – their greed for what Caesar might have bequeathed them, and the anger he is whipping up in them against the murderers of Caesar.

In a more positive vein, you might say something like: 'I was very excited when I saw that there *is* a way for us to get the product out to the customer quicker. I think you will be excited too when you realize that the new system will also cut your paperwork by about half.'

THE INTERNATIONAL ARENA: STORIES

Reselect the telling details

We suggested earlier that you should only supply the evocative key ideas when you tell a story – leaving your listener's imagination to provide the rest.

When you are working *across a culture gap* you should take nothing for granted; ideas that conveyed themselves in oblique references at home might have to be spelled out more laboriously when you are playing away.

Watch your language

This message is for you if you give presentations in English to non-English speakers, as is now so common in international business.

'Redundancy' is an important effect in language. Simply put, it means that an awful lot of what we say is unnecessary and repetitious. Often this is a good thing: if we build a lot of redundancy into our speech, we allow our listener to relax a little – he can follow the gist of what we are saying without concentrating on each individual word.

Often, when we tell a well-rehearsed anecdote, we use words much more economically, and try not to repeat ourselves. Often, the key idea in a story – like the punch-line in a joke – is expressed in very terse, Saxon language. Often, members of the audience who are more comfortable with Latinate formulations are left out in the cold.

The trick here is to select one or two members of the audience whom you know, or suspect, to be rather weak in English. Watch them closely during your presentation, especially when you are telling a story. If their eyes narrow or their shoulders go up in a shrug, it is a sign that they have just missed something. You should pause, and rephrase your last idea:

> and we certainly weren't going to let them get away with that! We decided to make sure it was impossible for them.

> but the decision was made, and there was no going back on it. We had to continue with the strategy.

> and we thought Paris to Nice in four hours was pretty good going. We were very satisfied with our progress.

You will often see a little smile of relief, or even a nod of gratitude.

Casual references that might not mean much when you're away from home

We have said a lot in this chapter about *leaving the audience to fill in the details*.

Within our home cultures, we use common points of reference to create quick settings in our listeners' minds: 'You know what it's like when you get on a tube train full of people who are soaked with rain, and half of them carrying umbrellas?'

Sometimes these little touches fall flat when you make your presentation to a group of 'foreigners'.

For the Swedish travelling to Britain:

❑ Deep-snow driving techniques

❑ Escaping from a hole in a frozen lake

❑ Why bedroom curtains should be black

For the British visiting Sweden:

❑ Anything to do with cricket

❑ Writing to your MP

❑ Playing devil's advocate

The audience can easily lose the thread of what you are saying while trying to puzzle out the meaning of such behaviour.

What this means to you

Your own strong convictions, your own natural power as a communicator, the expressive range of the hundreds of little muscles in your face: these can be channelled by training, and positive results come very quickly.

When you are preparing a presentation, keep returning to the question: 'Why am I doing it this way instead of writing a letter or making a phone call or sending a broadcast e-mail?'

The answer must have something to do with *human contact*. In business, human contact is an expensive waste of time unless it makes communication better.

So make it human. Allow your emotions to show.

THE INTERNATIONAL ARENA: EMOTION

Get your sincerity at the right pitch

When a Frenchman shrugs at your suggestion, and says 'Why not?', he might appear dismissive or even contemptuous. Yet he is quite possibly giving wholehearted endorsement to your proposal, in his oblique French way. In the same situation, a North German is likely to say directly: 'I give my whole-hearted endorsement to your suggestion.'

This is why the German stereotype of the French is 'creative but feckless', while the French sometimes find the Prussians to be leaden, predictable and literal-minded.

Similarly, when an American speaks earnestly in praise of his company: 'We put our customer first, at ABC, and we have the know-how to make fine products', the Englishman across the table winces: it isn't really done to beat the drum that way.

The Norwegian habitually undersells his company and its offer.

More important than the words you use are:

1. *Facial expression.* Little to worry about here. Most facial expressions carry pretty universal meanings in the developed world. Smiling a lot is seen in some Slavic countries as a bit simple-minded, but in any country, a far greater mistake is to keep your face cold and immobile – which signals lack of enthusiasm wherever you are.

2. *Tone of voice*. English, well-spoken from the platform, is one of the most expressive languages in terms of voice colour, pitch and tempo. Use the full range of expression, especially by placing great emphasis on the key ideas.

3. *Body language*. There is plenty of specialist literature about regional differences in the meaning of hand and finger movements. Safest on the presentation platform: hands in sight at all times, and gestures made with an open palm, fingers together. The frequency and energy of gestures varies greatly, with the Japanese seeming scarcely to move at all, and the South-Italians demonstrating traffic control techniques. If you come from Napoli, try not to flap your hands too wildly ten centimetres from the noses of the people in the front row. If you come from Osaka, try to inject a little animation before the final bow.

4

How can you draw your listener into your story?

I can listen for ages when someone is talking about me. After about two hours I begin to discern that the speaker is possessed of a great inner beauty.

You can buy clever audio cassettes for children these days, where the recording studio inserts the name of the recipient onto the tape:

Cecily decided to escape while the giant was asleep. She tip-toed to the mouth of the cave. The giant opened one eye and roared, 'Where do you think you're going, Cecily?'

Cecily, of course, just can't get enough of this stuff. It has

You-appeal

'Working' the audience

We assume now that you have captured your audience's attention (as in Chapter 1); they know the presentation is directed at them, and they are prepared to listen and to trust you. You have one or two excellent visuals ready, and a lively, memorable story or analogy to bring the idea to life.

Your job now is to hold their attention, and to help them to 'possess your idea'.

Most of this chapter is concerned with techniques of *persuasion*, well along the axis from the starting-point of *information*.

Yet even when seduction is far from your mind – when your purpose is simply to deliver the data – your audience will respond much more positively if you remember to slant the information their way, giving it

You-orientation

'YOU' IN INFORMATIVE PRESENTATIONS

When you set out to give a purely informative presentation, your audience presumably has a desire which matches: they wish to *gather* information.

We have all suffered at the hands of the speaker who thought it was good enough simply to read out the text he originally wrote for publication in print, or the college lecturer who delivers the same lecture series, from the same notes, year after year.

Yet even the college lecturer recognizes, as examination time approaches, that the students are more alert if he says, 'You might bear this in mind during your Solid State Physics/18th-Century Literature paper next week.'

When you are making a presentation, it is really just good manners to point out from time to time how your material is relevant to your listeners. More important, it is by pointing out the relevance that you help them to lodge the ideas in their memories.

> Many of you would be here, halfway up the vertical axis, giving you a figure of 17 per cent if we read across to the curve.

or

> I've chosen an example of how our services operate in a big city setting, since I know most of you live in and around Milan.

or

> You're all doctors and scientists, and probably haven't concerned yourselves much with questions of financial management – so far! But when they come to you in a few months and ask you to start taking budgetary responsibility, you'd be wise to concentrate on just a few key variables. For example...

Many speakers are afraid of overdoing this 'you' business; they think it seems forced or cheap. In fact, audiences have a very high tolerance for such direct appeals to their selfishness. Of course, it can become laboured if you try to couch *everything* you say in terms of 'you' and 'yours'.

There are three times when the 'you' content should be high:

❑ at the beginning of your presentation (see Chapter 1)
❑ when you are delivering the central, most important points, and
❑ whenever you sense that you are in danger of losing contact with your audience.

The first two should be dealt with at the preparation or writing stage; the third is a question of improvisation. A good speaker has a special mode of thinking, a kind of four-wheel drive which he can engage at a moment's notice. When he does, virtually everything he says is couched in 'you-language', and he is gratified to see his audience move forward a centimetre in their seats.

Exercise

Express the following ideas so that the words 'you', 'your' and 'yours' appear as often as possible. Your audience is a group of physical education teachers in their last week of training:

1. In all fitness training situations, the safety element is paramount.

2. When safety criteria have been met, it is time to consider the effectiveness of each training programme.

3. The personal attitude of the student is a crucial factor; training programme design should always take it into account.

4. For example, it is a mistake to set the student ambitious targets in the early days of training, if there is a danger that motivation might slip later. This is known as 'programming for failure'.

5. PE teachers succeed when they have the confidence of the students, individually and as a team. Setting achievable targets is the key to their confidence.

Of course we are here coming close to basic sales technique. The further you move along our *Inform–Persuade* axis, the more selling you are doing. And the more often you should say

> you

'YOU' IN PERSUASIVE PRESENTATIONS

A tourist guide at the Tower of London, or a gunnery instructor in the Navy, has a pre-selected, ready-defined audience: these tourists want a little colourful history, a few family jokes, and time to take photographs; these sailors want to be technically perfect, safe and perhaps get promoted.

These are classic 'telling' situations. When it comes to 'selling' you have to do a lot more advance thinking about your audience.

Who are they?

Why are they here?

Find out who they are

Ask colleagues, secretaries, customers, suppliers, competitors, friends. Think hard and read up on their background culture, the commercial environment they work in, the character and habits of the key players.

Get a clear picture of their sex, age, social class, education, functions, positions, expertise, experience, expectations, goals, fears, families, enemies, hobbies, tastes, etc.

What are the relationships within the audience group? Are there any in-jokes? Who already knows the thrust of your argument, and who is yet ignorant? If you are hoping for a decision, how will it be made?

Once you have identified the decision-makers, it is even more important to find out what makes them tick:

> If you would work any man, you must either know his nature or fashions, and so lead him; or his ends, and so persuade him; or his weaknesses and disadvantages, and so awe him; or those that have an interest in him, and so govern him.

Francis Bacon, 1597

Exercise

Picture yourself manning a stand at The Boat Show. In the tank before you floats your company's latest product, a cabin cruiser with all sorts of features and gadgets, and a slightly souped-up version of your well-respected engine.

Your sales literature is bland – a lot of photographs of the boat in pretty locations, and tables of technical specs. No people in the pictures.

You have various systems for making payment 'easy', but long before you get to that stage you have to convince any potential purchaser that this is *the* boat.

Which of the boat's features will you choose to emphasize as each customer agrees to climb aboard? How will you translate what is only a physical feature into a real, personal benefit for him?

At 10.30 you are visited by a family – father, mother, girl of 10 and boy of 8. At 11.15, a well-dressed man in his mid-20s. Just after lunch, a retired gentleman.

By afternoon tea, you might have sold separate cabins and a bit of privacy to the father, or safety equipment and peace of mind to the mother.

The young man might have thought about the powerful engine note as a mating signal.

The elderly gent, a fisherman perhaps, might have been lured by the copious storage space for his equipment, and the freezer for all the fish he dreams of catching.

Find out why they are here

Assume that your listener is coming to your presentation more or less voluntarily. (It is hard to deal with listeners who are only there 'because my boss told me to come'.)

Ask yourself:

❑ What have I got that might satisfy his real need?

❑ What have I got that might tickle his appetite?

❑ What have I got that might enhance his self-esteem?

Need

If a man is cold, hungry and weary, you do not have to make a clever presentation to persuade him to sit by the fire, eat and sleep.

The psychologist Maslow called this most basic level of human needs 'hygiene factors'. One important idea is this: if your audience is unsatisfied in some area of 'hygiene', then they will not be ready to listen to your persuasive messages in less essential areas.

Senior managers in a failing company facing bankruptcy will pay little attention to your proposals for a new staff appraisal system. A group of production engineers who are running behind schedule installing a new assembly line will not be very interested in your presentation about a new lubricant. More mundanely, an audience that is worried about missing the last bus home will not listen very closely to your suggestions for improving parent–teacher communication in the junior school.

But if the company is healthy, the assembly line is running smoothly, or the transport home is all laid on, then your staff appraisal system, new lubricant, or educational proposal can be presented *as a basic need*.

> *Staff appraisal:* 'You have often said that people are your key resource. Surely it is essential to take stock of that resource and deploy it effectively.'

> *New lubricant:* 'Increasing maintenance intervals is the most obvious way of increasing productivity – which you all name as a top priority. Now oil changes are the most basic maintenance routine.'

> *Educational proposal:* 'We've got ten minutes before the bus leaves. It's been a useful evening so far, no doubt, but we still haven't tackled the most crucial question of all. We all, parents and teachers, want the children to succeed, and we all agree that close collaboration between school and home is absolutely fundamental.'

The history of the West this century is littered with examples of goods and services that have moved from the realms of fantasy to a reality reserved for the very rich, and from there to the category of everyday necessity for Mr Average: Cars, washing machines, holidays, insurance, etc.

Appetite

Or, as some would have it, *greed* – for money, comfort, long life, pleasant sensations, beautiful things. All these you *could* get by without.

The big airlines know that 80 per cent of their revenue comes from 20 per cent of their clients – the regular business travellers.

Watch how they try to retain those customers with wider seats, gorgeous flight attendants, a glass of champagne, special facilities at airports. To avoid charges of sybaritism, a secondary message is sometimes appended: 'So that you can arrive refreshed and ready for serious decision-making.'

In your presentation, if your product or service is definitely in the luxury category, sell it accordingly:

> Perhaps you feel that, in celebration of a spectacularly successful year, your office Christmas party should be something special.

> There are sun-creams and there are sun-creams. Now if you really want the best...

> What I've shown you already would probably give you what you really need – at a basic level. But if you are ready to spend just a little more, and have your front driveway the envy of the street...

This last example is important in Maslow terms. Since man is a social animal, a very powerful set of drives exists around 'good standing in the community'.

Keeping up with the Joneses has been recognized as a social force since the 1950s – the first time that ostentation was an option for any but a tiny minority of people.

Many people are prepared to suffer minor privations in order to keep up appearances – cheap lodgings in a smart part of town, living on bread and cheese for six days in order to join friends for dinner in a restaurant on Friday evening, and even suffering travel delays in order to be sure of a Business Class seat.

Self-esteem

In fact Maslow called it 'self-actualization': the point at the top of the staircase of motivation. All basic needs – food, shelter, safety – have been met. Good fortune and hard work have brought a lot of luxuries. Social standing is assured, the children have done well at school, and life seems good.

What is left? The motivation to feel one's life has been worthwhile, one's potential fulfilled.

An appeal at this level can be particularly useful when addressing senior management:

> A mature view needs to be taken.

> If what you want is a strong five years of stable growth, in order to focus on big strategic issues...

The decision is not an easy one, which is why it is for you to make. Finally the decision will probably be made from instinct and experience.

What this means to you

The more you find out about your audience, the more chance you stand of triggering a response when you make your presentation.

You should ask yourself if your 'offer' will appeal to them at the level of *need*, *appetite* or *self-esteem*.

Large corporations invest in market research to identify emerging demands in the population. Then they adapt their product range and promotion – the offer – to suit, and meet that demand. On a personal scale, you should follow the same procedure. Then,

❏ If they really *need* what you are offering, and you have no competitors, just to explain it clearly will be enough.

❏ If you are trying to tempt their *appetite*, with an attractive but unnecessary treat, highlight the attractions and help them to see this luxury item as a real *need*.

❏ If your proposal will boost their *self-esteem* in some way, emphasize this aspect in addition to the rational arguments.

So far in this chapter we have assumed that the audience is quite interested in the information you have to give them. Further, we have supposed that they are ready to listen more or less sympathetically to your proposal.

We are often asked 'how can I overcome resistance, even hostility, in my audience?'

There is a problem with the way that question is framed: the word 'overcome'. It suggests a frontal attack in force. As a presenter, you do not want to invade your audience's territory, you want to settle it.

ADDRESSING A HOSTILE AUDIENCE

Think of your proposal as a vector – a line of force moving in a particular direction:

The hostility of your audience might seem impenetrable:

Clearly it will do no good to push straight ahead. (Anyway, how can you? By shouting louder?)

Find a vector that's going your way

Your listener's perceptions of the world are certainly more complex than one fat black **NO !**
   Some of his vectors are certainly

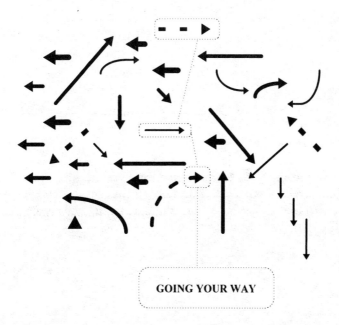

GOING YOUR WAY

Sometimes the situation really is hopeless – Galileo trying to persuade the *curia* that the earth was spinning around the sun, for example. Or trying to press shellfish soup on a dinner guest who is allergic to seafood.

In less dramatic cases, there is usually a 'way in'. Teenagers often try to use it:

Teenager: Dad, you know you're always saying we spend too much on bus fares.

Father: No, you can't have a motor bike.

Once you have identified the vector that will carry your listener in your direction, you need to handle the situation delicately.

Exploit the vectors carefully

In an appendix at the back of this book is Abraham Lincoln's Gettysburg Address, the very short speech that was a turning point in American history.

The northern side was beginning to tire in the Civil War, and Lincoln spent days preparing a speech, for delivery in a war cemetery, to inspire them to continue.

The vector he chose to ride was this: you know that many good men have died; their bodies are all around us. We owe it to them to continue the fight; otherwise it is all a terrible waste.

Lincoln follows a classical model for persuading his audience:

1. *Confluence* Tell them your idea flows in the same direction as theirs. Lincoln begins by saying, 'our fathers brought forth upon this continent a new nation' – and we wouldn't want to go against our father's wishes, would we?

2. *Reason* Choose your first logical base carefully, and develop a clear argument from that. If the American Constitution really was 'dedicated to the proposition that all men are created equal', then the rest of Lincoln's argument follows clearly.

3. *Participation* Get the audience involved in doing something. The words *we, our* and *us* appear 15 times in Lincoln's speech: 'We are met... We have come... It is for us the living... to be dedicated... to the unfinished work.'

Exercise

Design a line of argument, observing the rules of *confluence, reason* and *participation* for the following situations:

❏ Persuading a partner to take a holiday in a country he or she does not like

❏ Convincing a colleague to do some of your work for you

❏ Talking a traffic warden out of giving you a ticket

Support your argument with concrete evidence

It even adds a little to the power of Lincoln's argument that he says, 'Four score and seven years ago' rather than just 'a long time back'.

Justifying his witch hunts in the USA, Senator Joe McCarthy was fond of claims like: 'There are 205 card-carrying communists in the State Department.'

Be prepared to deliver facts and figures.

Add a little passion

We dealt with the use of emotion at some length in an earlier chapter. If you really care about what you are proposing, let it show.

Be open about it

Many people are uncomfortable with the idea of persuasion: 'If I use tricks to make people change their opinions, then I am manipulating them and that's wrong.'

It can only be wrong if you do it in an underhand way. Instead, come out into the daylight:

'I've thought a lot about your situation, and I think I can convince you.'

'There is one factor in your life which means you should consider my proposal very seriously.'

'Clearly you will have several arguments against my idea, but let's consider the aspects you approve of.'

What this means to you

If you want to *persuade* your listener, you should find that vector in his make-up which most clearly coincides with your own purposes.

Then give it a series of gentle nudges – during a single presentation if you must, over a series if you can.

At every stage, use all your other skills as a presenter to give your strategy the best chance of working.

Finally, try a little honesty.

THE INTERNATIONAL ARENA

'You'

If you are facing a mixed-nationality group, it helps if you can provide selected examples to bring your material home to them:

'So this is where the *Independent* fits in the socio-political situation. For comparison, I've marked positions here for *Le Monde* and *Frankfurter Allgemeine Zeitung*'

(If an Italian then asks for help, and you know nothing of the Italian press, somebody else in the audience will probably come to your rescue. Then you have a discussion. Wonderful.)

Need, appetite, self-esteem

Your message will need careful modification as you move away from home-base.

An audience in Rome might respond very positively if you appeal to their sense of privilege – 'You deserve the most expensive, and everyone knows this is it'.

The same message would go down badly in New Zealand, where it is not normal to be ostentatious. And among the new rich in Russia or China, there is no need to talk about people *deserving* their luxuries.

Persuasion: conflict or confluence?

Similarly, different cultures have different ideas on manipulation and bullying.

It has been observed, for example, that many Swedes lack 'the killer instinct' in business – that they are all naive, blue-eyed honesty. They have been conditioned by their culture and now view 'persuasion with a dash of psychology' as 'shameful dirty tricks'.

If a Swedish audience suspects that you are attempting insidious manipulation, they will quickly turn against you and switch their minds off.

In America, conversely, shrewd and determined tactics are part of everyday business life.

5

Can you really change your listener's beliefs?

So you have established your credentials, employed well-chosen devices to attract your audience's attention and lodge your idea in their memories, and laced the whole thing with lots of you-appeal.

Now the deeper question:

Will they see things differently from now on?

We have seen Mark Antony several times already, grabbing his audience's attention and entering their right brains by the use of strong images.

Shortly before his great speech he states that he has a specific purpose in mind: 'Woe to the hand that shed this costly blood!' – the turncoat assassin, Brutus, must pay the price of his crime. The means is to be 'domestic fury and fierce civil strife', and Mark Antony has decided that the Roman mob should get things rolling.

People remember his speech for the way he handles his message to the mob: 'Caesar was *not* an ambitious tyrant. He loved you and you should avenge him!'

He drips the idea into them gradually, letting them work things out for themselves – but always with his guidance. Then, when finally he starts to give his message to them directly, they recognize it as something they already 'know'. And now here is this excellent fellow telling them that he believes it, too. It must be true. Down with Brutus! (By the way, history shows us that large audiences can be easier to sway than small, critical groups. In large numbers, people tend to think, feel and act uniformly. Shakespeare learned this from the classical authors, and from observation.)

At the *persuasion* end of the spectrum, you are trying to *man-*

age people's beliefs. If we accept that as a general objective, then the challenge is

> **to make your message serve your objective**

and

> **to handle your message effectively**

Keep your objective clearly in mind

When you are making your presentations, there are many contradictory temptations:

- ❏ to stay on safe ground, or to try something new and daring
- ❏ to fill the time available; to make it nice and short so we can have a pleasant lunch
- ❏ to exaggerate small matters for dramatic effect; to understate important points because they seem so obvious

These activities all have their place, *provided they are serving your objective.*

Everything that carries you in the right direction offers a good setting for your central message.

Each time you state your central message, in whatever form, it should consistently accelerate the movement towards the objective.

Let your message work for itself

When *Lego*, the children's building toy, was first introduced, the starter pack was a box with all sizes and colours of bricks, plus a few doors and windows. Supplementary packs could then be bought: more specialized bricks, garage doors and so forth. These supplementary packs were priced to be just about right for an aunt to buy for Little Billy's birthday.

Some years later, *Lego* changed the nature of the supplementary packs. Each one could now be used to only one purpose: to make a helicopter, or to make a telephone kiosk.

Sales among aunts rocketed. They had never really liked the previous arrangement, because Little Billy used to mix the bricks from Auntie's birthday present in with all the other bricks, and even lose some under the sofa. Now she could buy him a nice helicopter to assemble and put on the playroom shelf where she could see it on her next visit.

The advertising and point-of-sale material left the message unspoken. It was better to let Auntie work it out for herself.

We are often asked by people we are coaching: 'Should I tell my audience at the start what it is I hope to convince them of?'

We say yes, if it seems appropriate. The *Lego* company was quite open about wanting people to buy the product. So you can tell your audience: 'I hope to convince you that I have the solution to your problem.'

Conversely, do not over explain the solution to the problem. Permit your listener to say to himself: 'Quite smart of me to work this bit out.'

What it means to you

Leave a bit of work for the audience to do themselves.

An audience that has arrived at its own conclusions is more thoroughly convinced of those ideas – their 'own' ideas – even if you have helped the ideas to germinate.

Make your audience reach out for your idea

Antony: But here's a parchment, with the seal of Caesar... Which, pardon me, I do not mean to read.

The mob of course, is soon screaming for Mark Antony to read Caesar's last will out to them.

With more subtle audiences, these pantomime tactics might not work. But is it really such a different ploy when the speaker says:

'I've studied the situation long and hard, and I've got a few novel ideas, but I don't think I should push them at you...'

or

'There's one other piece of evidence which, for most people, is a clincher – but most of you have probably already guessed...'

What this means to you

Don't just *give* your ideas to the audience.

Set a puzzle for them, let them work on it, suggest you have an answer, let them ask for it.

Dig a hole, push them in, offer to help them out. They can't refuse.

This is the moment for a little flattery: 'There you are, you see! You got out of the hole!'

Convert your key points into rhetorical questions

In the first half of Mark Antony's big scene, he asks a number of very controlled questions:

> Did this in Caesar seem ambitious?

> Was this ambitious?

> What withholds you then to mourn for him?

> Will you be patient? Will you stay awhile?

> You will compel me then to read the will?

> Shall I descend? And will you give me leave?

Kind souls, what weep you, when you but behold Our Caesar's vesture wounded?

Holding up Caesar's tattered, bloodied toga, and *still* not having read out the will, Antony begins to drip in the idea of mutiny.

Rhetorical questions are very powerful, and equally risky. Everybody is embarrassed when they go wrong.

Orator: Are you mice, or men?
Audience: Squeak!

or

Orator: Have you ever dreamed of owning your own cabin cruiser?
Audience: Not really, no. Can't say I have.

or

Orator: When was the last time you felt really financially secure?
Audience: Last month when I got my pay-cheque.

But correctly used, they draw your audience in:

'Now, how many of our big customers – Category A here – do you suppose were down in Category D five years ago?'

'Is there any reason to postpone your thinking about the long-term future?'

'Why not set resources aside for this project, while we have those resources to hand?'

Handling rhetorical questions

	FORM OF QUESTION	WHAT HAPENS
CLOSED		
	... isn't it?	They nod
	... weren't they?	
	... couldn't you?	You get contact and confirmation
	Can we...?	They say 'Yes' or 'No'
	Do you...?	
	Have they...?	You get more 'buy-in' from them
	From these options, which...?	They voice opinons, but you maintain control
	What...?	They might contribute; they might not
	When...?	
	Where...?	You need an emergency procedure in
	Who...?	case of horrible silence
	How...?	(*eg* 'Most people say at this point...')
	Why...?	Start of a discussion
	Any more ideas about...?	You should now chair the meeting
OPEN		

What this means to you

Look at the chapter title at the head of the opposite page. Is a statement the only way of making a point?

Exercise

Convert these statement into rhetorical questions. (Your audience is a group of German and American managers on their way to work in a joint venture in China.)

* It will not be easy to graft Western management styles onto local working practices.
* Local managers will feel resentful... especially if you are planning 40 per cent staff cuts.
* Western organization development consultants know little about the varying cultures of China.
* You should consider, as a first step, employing local management consultants to advise you.

Sssh!

It takes time for your listeners to work on the ideas you are offering them, especially if you do not spell all the answers out.

❑ Don't put one question inside another, like Russian dolls:

Orator: I ask you: Is the time right for a new policy? Do we have the right managers to implement such policies? Where are we to find such people?

Audience: Er... yes, no, and... what was the last question?

❑ Pause for a long time after each question, leaving your listeners alone with their thoughts.

❑ Resist the temptation to answer the question yourself.

❑ Watch the audience carefully: you can often read the moment when they have found the answer within themselves. They nod, or blink, or change position in their seats.

What this means to you

When you have posed a question, give your audience time to think about the answer.

You needn't wait for them to speak the answer; often you can say:

'I hope that has set you thinking. Now let's move on to our next point.'

Build up your audience's confidence in you by maintaining your credibility

Spending all this time on the edge of their seats, the audience will need reassurance that they are in good hands.

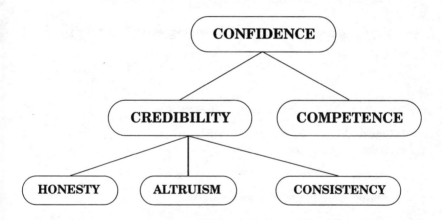

Their confidence in you is based on your personal *credibility* – your honesty, your altruism and your consistency. It is also dependent on what they see as your *competence* – your command of the subject, and your power to make things happen.

We return to the question of *competence* in a later section, which is devoted to Question-and-Answer sessions; this is where your competence will be probed.

Personal *credibility* is of course vital for politicians, and it is hard for them to maintain in a world of electioneering ups and downs, media distortion, and promises broken for whatever reason.

They ring the changes on *honesty*, *altruism* and *consistency*. If, at a given moment, they appear weak in one of these virtues, they make a lot of noise about one of the others.

OK, I lied (0/10 for honesty) – *BUT*

I did it to help poor people (10/10 for altruism); or

I was in pursuit of my single, overriding objective (10/10 for consistency)

I was looking after my own interests (0/10 for altruism) – *BUT*

I have openly published all the details (10/10 for honesty); or

My actions were in line with our strategy (10/10 for consistency)

I have changed my mind (0/10 for consistency) – *BUT*

New circumstances compel me to do so (10/10 for honesty); or

I fight on for the same great cause (10/10 for altruism)

Next time you see a politician on the spot, watch out for this technique.

What this means to you

To build up the audience's confidence in you, you need to maintain your credibility. Try to be:

* Honest, truthful, accurate and respectful of facts

* Altruistic – or at least generous and constructive

* Consistent, reliable and thorough

If you manage most of this most of the time, you will be seen as a healthy source of good ideas that can safely be imbibed.

Distil your message

The expression 'central message' is used in this book to describe that point in a presentation when you deliver, in a few well-chosen words, the main idea that you want your audience to take away with them.

Many people remember the ironical drumbeat in Mark Antony's speech:

For Brutus is an honourable man, So are they all; all honourable men.

But Brutus says he was ambitious, And Brutus is an honourable man (repeated three times)

The fate of Brutus is sealed when Antony singles him out as the vilest of all the conspirators. By agreement, they all stabbed Caesar, but the 'honourable' Brutus was Caesar's favourite. Antony here delivers his central message:

This was the most unkindest cut of all.

HOW TO MAKE A GOOD CENTRAL MESSAGE

❏ Use 'Saxon', not Latin vocabulary. Churchill's challenge of 'Blood, toil, tears and sweat' is better than 'blood, labour, tears and sweat', and much better than 'blood, toil, tears and perspiration'.

❏ Employ active, not passive constructions. Don't say 'This contract will be won by our sales force', say 'Our sales force will win this contract'.

❏ Set up contrasts, 'It isn't cheap, but it'll save you money in the long run.' ('I come to bury Caesar, not to praise him.')

❏ Use terms close to your listeners: 'If some guy's got a dollar he didn't work for, some guy's worked for a dollar he didn't get.' (Communism explained to American truck drivers)

❏ Employ a traditional trick:

THREE-PART LIST: Liberté, Egalité, Fraternité
                            Hook, line and sinker

ALLITERATION: Back to Basics
                            Form Follows Function

BOTH TOGETHER: Veni, vidi, vici
                            Kirche, Kinder, Küche

THE INTERNATIONAL ARENA

Every civilization has surely had its own style book for public speakers, and its own rules of debate. Yet there are many universals.

A cinema audience watching Marlon Brando's wonderful Mark Antony deliver the speech over the dead Julius Caesar is watching an American, 'method'-trained actor recorded on film, delivering a speech written by an Englishman (Shakespeare) four centuries ago for a very different style of actor, closely based on accounts by Roman historians of what happened that day in Rome a millennium before. The real Mark Antony was trained in rhetoric according to even older Greek principles.

The cinema experience works today because

❏ in all times, and in all places, audiences have reacted in broadly the same ways to well-shaped, well-delivered messages;

❏ in all times and in all places, clever speakers have designed and transmitted their messages according to the same broad basic principles.

Evoke, don't dictate

The first messages of this chapter:

> Keep your objective clearly in mind
> Let your message work for itself
> Make your audience reach out for your idea
> Convert your key points into rhetorical questions
> Sssh!

all hold true wherever in the world you might be addressing an audience.

Audiences from the old Communist world are accustomed to being harangued and bludgeoned into a set of prescribed beliefs. Audiences of Americans who failed to go on after high school are used to being given answers without first being provoked into much thought.

An audience of Siberian oil engineers or of American ice-cream salesmen might be puzzled for a moment when you allow them to range freely in search of their own conclusions. You will need to make it very clear that you are asking a question: 'I am now going to write a question up on the board and ask you what you think the answer might be'. They will quickly take to the process – and perhaps remember you as the speaker who handled his message in a new and better way.

Choose the right man for the job

On the question of *confidence* and *credibility*, it must be said that deep cultural programming exists.

It might be very difficult for an audience of senior Japanese executives to take seriously proposals made by a boy of 29.

An audience of Iranian men might find it hard to listen seriously to a woman with long blonde hair.

Watch your language

Our point about the power of Saxon words ('killing' and 'eating' rather than 'assassination' and 'nourishment') is true in Northern Europe and generally in the USA.

If you are delivering your presentation in a country with a Romance language base (French, Italian, Spanish) your audience will find it easier to digest Latin-based terms.

> 'We just didn't sell as many as we'd hoped to'

should be translated into

> 'Unfortunately, we did not achieve our objective with regard to sales.'

Please note: this does not mean resorting to fancy management jargon.

Which has the ring of truth about it:

> There's no market for it
> *or*
> Nobody wants to buy it

> We're currently in the pilot phase
> *or*
> We're still playing with the idea?

6

How to build and deliver your argument

STRUCTURE AND PACING

You have thought about your audience – particularly:

❏ their level of knowledge (in the case of an *informative* presentation); or

❏ their needs and appetites (in the case of a more *persuasive* performance).

You have selected very stringently from the information available; pared the ideas down to an effective minimum.

The question now is how to impose some *structure* on the material.

To give some *structure* to this chapter, we will move along our spectrum from *inform* to *persuade*, pausing about half way along in an area which we will call *teach*, to see what we can learn from speakers in university lecture halls and high school classrooms.

Go from general to particular

In a purely informative presentation, your starting-point is determined by the level of knowledge of your audience. How much do they already know? OK, we'll start from there.

If you are addressing a split-level audience, including experts, amateurs and ignorami, you have a problem. Aim for the middle, perhaps saying:

'Many of you already know this, but please be patient while I set the scene.'

Then *set the scene*. Give them the general context – the broad background; put them in the picture.

They need time to switch on and warm up their information storage system. In each mind there is a library of many sections and many, many shelves, and if your new piece of information arrives without a good bibliographical label, it will be classified wrongly (lost), or even rejected as unclassifiable (forgotten).

Then say:

'Within this context, I'd like to focus now on one particular item.'

Deliver the goods. At this point it is right to say:

'I'll be concentrating on the most striking aspects, but there will be more detail available in handouts at the end.'

(You have made a careful selection, so as not to swamp them during the presentation, but the 'experts' will have an appetite for more.)

Give the audience a *route map*:

'I'll be talking for about fifteen minutes, and there will be time after that for your questions. I'll be covering three main points – x, y and z'

And plant *signposts* along the way:

'So that covers x. If there are no immediate questions I'll move on to y.'

'So much for y. Now, turning our attention to z.'

Keep showing them how the whole thing fits together. 'And', 'also' and 'furthermore' are very weak links – they sound like bits of a list that could go on forever. Say rather:

'This clearly means that…'

'And so we can see…'

'Naturally this leads us to the next item, which is…'

When you have finished with the specifics, say:

'Now let's remind ourselves of where all this fits in the bigger picture.'

Then give a broad-brush *summary*. It will help your audience commit the whole thing to memory – check that the newly arrived information is on the right shelf, and correctly cross-referenced.

Your job is to inform, and help the audience remember; you are not a stand-up comic, eternally springing surprises, and delivering his gags so quickly that nobody can remember 20 per cent an hour later. Your audience has limited powers of concentration, and you owe it to them to make sure that they know where they are every step of the way.

When you lay out a written report, you make full use of *chap-*

ter *titles*, *headings*, and *paragraph breaks*, so that your reader can find his way around the text – and find his place again if he puts it down for a while.

Life is tougher for your listener at a presentation. He can't run his eye back up the page to see where he got lost; you as a speaker don't come equipped with a rewind button. Give him all the help you can.

Measure their interest

In the 15th century, knowledge was a rare, precious and fascinating commodity. People survived in a dearth of news and information about the wide world. When a speaker came with fresh data – a visitor to the village, a soldier returned from the war, a guest from a sister abbey – they were rapt.

The same level of attention might be found today when an internationally famous professor speaks to a tickets-only audience on a special occasion.

Otherwise, audiences in the industrialized world (your audiences, probably) are swamped with information. They overdosed long before you took the platform.

They don't really want you to give them too much more.

What this means to you

Decide how important and interesting your information is for your audience. Be honest.

If you can truly say that they are enthusiastic about what you can deliver, then fine. Just let them have it. On the other hand, you might come to realize that what you have to offer is only moderately enticing.

In such cases, you should spend a few minutes at the start – in a separate, persuasive presentation – convincing them that the material you have is worth focusing on for a few minutes.

Either way, the information should then be delivered in a well-organized, clearly labelled package.

Select the information to suit your audience's world

One of the present authors was involved with a company which had taken on a large group of immigrant guest workers, and housed them in guest accommodation blocks (or 'barrack-sheds', as the workers insisted on calling them).

A senior manager addressed them early in their stay, with a motivational message about the company's plans for growth, and the important part they had to play in those plans. He left it to a junior to give them the workaday stuff, like:

❑ where to complain about the food in the canteen;

❑ where to complain about the toilet facilities; and

❑ the rules about women visitors to the barracks.

Months later, after experiencing interventions from various executives, they still remembered the junior's presentation, and referred to him as 'the only clever man in the company'.

Start with a bang

Even when your information is well-organized and relevant, there will be times when your audience needs perking up a bit.

It is rather dreary to begin with 'This all started in 1878...' or 'Quite a lot of people have installed equipment like this without too much difficulty...'.

Speak about the here and now, or even better about the immediate future, at the start of your presentation. Tempt the appetite with one specific, telling detail.

'Next week sees the culmination of eight years of development'

'My next-door neighbour is using this energy-saving system now, and it only took us a weekend to install it.'

A good press release follows these rules, as does the newspaper article which is based on the release. The aim is the same: to grab the reader's attention:

Borrow a technique from the press relations people

Make contact early

Let your audience know from the start that you intend to inter-act with them: 'Old Harry there was telling me in the bar ear-lier...'

> **Borrow from the night club compere**

Use high spots on the concentration curve

The concentration/retention span of an audience looks like this:

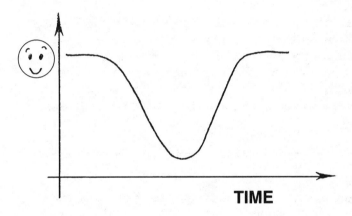

TIME

People absorb and retain the things they hear first and the things they hear last. They doze off in the middle. This is true of any speech lasting longer than five minutes.

The good teacher knows about the concentration/retention curve, and takes it into account. He gives his class the most use-ful information at the beginning of the lesson, and at the end.

> **Borrow from the good teacher**

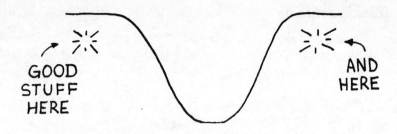

Of course, it is nice to create other major and minor attention peaks when you want them, by upping or cooling the tempo. Good teachers know about this, too.

Use your voice

Keep it up. A series of falling cadences sends people to sleep. A mumbling delivery makes you seem unsure of yourself, and undermines their confidence in your message.

At key moments, turn up the amplitude and the frequency, the dB and the Hz, the volume and the pitch. And remember all we said in the last chapter about the importance of pauses.

Exercise

Beginning with Monday, recite the days of the week aloud, injecting as much colour as you can.

Starting with January, do the same with the months of the year.

Change what they're looking at

Switch back and forth from whiteboard to flipchart to OHP to videobeam. The variety of stimulus helps your audience to stay alert.

Change the way *you* look. If you are good at histrionic gestures, we don't aim to teach you anything from the pages of a book. We are not talking about the ability to cry at will, or get under the skin of a character from Chekhov, but the knack of 'shifting register', from formal to relaxed, from static to demonstrative, from cool academic to cosy intimate.

If you are not a natural in this department, and you don't want to go to drama classes you can easily

- ❏ *Change your position on the stage*, moving left to right, front to back, coming out from behind the lectern.
- ❏ *Take some notes out of your pocket*, like Harold Macmillan, who used to fumble in his jacket pocket for a blank sheet of paper and 'refer to it' – in order to build up the tension.
- ❏ *Take your glasses off*, or screw your monocle in.
- ❏ *Sit down; stand up.*

Make the audience do something

Circumstances rarely permit you to have your audience rolling round on the floor or swinging from the rafters. Conference rooms rarely come equipped with sandpit or Wendy house. But for the sake of involvement, you should explore the limits of your setting. Get them to: clap hands; hold hands; empty their pockets; write an answer on a scrap of paper ('OK, now hands up everybody who guessed more than 35 per cent); close their eyes for a moment; open them and look at each other; stand up/sit down.

Tell a joke

We mean a 'joke' joke – the story with a punch-line. But only tell them if you really are a good teller of jokes, and if the joke in some way supports your general argument.

When you next tell a joke at a party, and the people laugh, look around you: are they *really* amused, or just being polite. Unless you are above-average funny, leave jokes out of your presentation. They will be painful for everybody.

Schoolteachers who tell bad jokes, or tell good jokes badly, are made aware of it by their pupils' groans. All too often in business, a senior manager who is bad at telling jokes insists nonetheless on telling them from the presentation platform. The sycophantic laughter of his subordinates is not a pleasant sound.

Remember that less is more

Be economical with your effects. A good teacher knows that basic hard work by the students is part of the learning process, and uses extra stimulation as an incentive. He does not make every lecture a 50-minute party.

Refer back to Chapter 2

Where we deal at length with the power of visuals, stories and emotions. A good picture, an engaging anecdote, or a blast of happiness or anger will wake the audience up a treat.

Colour-and-Movement, the child psychologists call it. It will snap your audience out of their revery, and bring them back to where they belong – attending your message.

What this means to you

Like the best teachers, you can manufacture a series of attention peaks during your presentation, by stimulating your audience's senses and imagination.

So we have moved from straight *information* to the world of *teaching*. Next, at the *persuasion* end of our scale, we find one of the most powerful *structures* available to the presenter.

We make everyday *decisions* like this:

Today I'm going to a meeting with a client, so it has to be the dark blue suit. Which shirt shall I wear?

I like the pale grey, but it's in the wash. Or I could wear the pink stripe, but I haven't got a tie to go with it... or... or

Fine, I'll wear the white one with the button-down collar.

Exercise

Think about other small decisions you have made recently within the same structure – your journey to work, perhaps, or what to give your mother for her birthday.

In *problem-solving conversations*, we say:

The kids are growing up now, and we're going to need an extra bedroom soon...

I suppose you could give up your study, and do your writing in the kitchen.

I don't fancy that... what about you working some overtime, so we can afford a bigger flat?

Or...

Or...

Good, then that's agreed. We look around the cheaper areas of town, to see if we can find a house with a bit more space for the same money.

In the nature of things, and especially when resources are limited, the resolution of the process is usually a compromise.

In *persuasive presentation*, it helps if you draw your audience along your decision path with you – almost as if you were letting them help you solve the problem.

Impose a strict structure on your argument

1. *Give them the necessary background:* This is the situation we are in...
2. *Show them that steps must be taken:* And this means a decision is due...
3. *Present the options:* So you could... or... or... or... (a realistic list)
4. *Evaluate the options:* On grounds of x... despite y... considering z...
5. *Make your proposal:* The clear choice is...

(Antony Jay, one of the best writers on presentation technique, trims this down to 'The 4 Ps': Position > Problem > Possibilities > Proposal.)

At each step in the process, your audience will be signalling agreement: 'Yes, that's the way it is... we follow your reasoning.'

That agreement with your logic is virtually the same as agreement with your proposal.

Build your structure close to your audience

The *evaluation* stage is vital; your audience must agree with your criteria.

If they have strong reasons (personal, emotional, political, cultural) for favouring one of your options, you cannot dismiss it casually:

> The idea of armed revolution, comrade Guevara, we reject on the grounds of common sense.

Priorities may differ from audience to audience, rendering some of your arguments weak or absurd:

> We favour the bus over the train, Mr Trump, on the grounds that it is cheaper.

Exercise

Here are six reasons why your boss should read this book. Rank them in order of importance as they would appear to him:

1. Sometimes people go to sleep in his presentations.

2. He likes reading management books.

3. He has been promising himself a refresher course in communication skills.

4. His visual aids are dull and boring.

5. He is nervous about making presentations.

6. He has been making the same three presentations for years.

THE INTERNATIONAL ARENA

Gesture

If you naturally use your arms and hands when you speak, you are in danger of giving offence – or at least causing amusement – unintentionally.

One finger in the air ('Listen to this!') suggests the erect male organ in many parts of the world.

Elsewhere, forefinger and thumb closed in a circle ('Perfect!') signify the female pudenda.

When you are making a presentation in some exotic spot – south of Milan or east of Vienna – don't jam your hands in your pockets for fear they will betray you. Just keep your hands open and your fingers together, relaxed and slightly cupped – the way they hang when you let your arms *drop* by your sides.

Now use these paddles for your gestures – pointing, beckoning, emphasizing.

Jokes

Jokes are very culture-specific.

Amusing anecdotes, a general light-hearted attitude, funny pictures: these things travel quite well.

But if you have a wealth of travelling salesman funnies, or shaggy dog stories, or Bob Hope one-liners, leave them at home.

QUESTION AND ANSWER SESSION

We promised to return to the question of *competence* – letting your audience know that you are in command of your material and aware of its implications.

The best time to consolidate your position in their eyes is during the Q & A session.

Have the right attitude

You have to work to build rapport with your audience; your presentation should not be like a monologue on the radio. (The audience might change stations.)

Many presenters manage contact quite well while the flow of ideas runs outwards from them to the audience – while they are in complete control. But some go to pieces – freeze, turn in on themselves, start talking nonsense – when the audience starts to fire questions: which is surely the time when a real, memorable dialogue should begin!

Your questions answered

'What if the question is silly and irrelevant?'

Such questions often stem from your questioner's view of the situation, as he struggles to try to make your ideas fit his world.

Often, such a question is an invitation: 'Would you please try once more to help me get a grip on your proposal?'

Rather than just answer the question in all its 'silly irrelevance', use the opportunity to explain your argument once again to the questioner, from a slightly different angle.

'Of course I can see how, from your standpoint, this is an important matter. Let's consider it in the context of the main point.'

What if the question is hostile?

Don't fight back. If you pick a fight with one audience member, you've picked a fight with them all.

Try to answer patiently – once. Then if the hostility continues, recognize it as such, and use the power of the group to your advantage, saying:

'I don't think I'm able to satisfy you on that right now. Perhaps we can get together and talk it out later. Now rather than waste everybody's time, I'd like to take another question.'

What if the questioner knows more than I do?

In a mixed level audience, some of them might be more expert than you in certain areas.

Sometimes in such circumstances the question is not really a question at all, but the means by which the 'questioner' displays his expertise to the audience: 'I wonder how much use you have made of Professor McGilbert's work on this'; 'Isn't that export sales figure a little low, if you take into account a probable drop in the Yen exchange rate against the dollar?'

Don't offer an answer: none is required. Just thank the questioner for his help.

What if I mishear the question?

If you are in any doubt, ask for an instant replay. It is very embarrassing to hear a presenter answering the wrong question.

What if I don't know the answer?

Say so. Then promise to find the answer as soon as possible, and send it to the questioner.

You will go up greatly in the audience's estimation.

Is there any way I can get ready for the Q & A session?

As with your presentation itself, preparation is more than half the battle.

A very clever or very lucky speaker can find a way to answer a question satisfactorily, *and* relate it back to his main message,

and use it as a means of improving relations with the audience –
all *apparently* spontaneously.

1. *Work out what the hot question is likely to be.* Build a trailer
   into your presentation: 'I won't dwell on the issue of x now; if
   any of you has a special interest, we can find time at the discussion stage.'

2. *Hook it back to your objective.* Don't go as far as the politician
   who ignores all the journalist's questions and just repeats
   and repeats his tub-thumping message again and again. But
   you *can* say: 'And if that answers your question, it also sheds
   further light on what we've seen throughout this discussion –
   namely that...'

3. *Arm yourself with another two or three ways of expressing
   your message.* If you use the same turn of phrase over and
   over again, your credibility falls. Ring the changes: 'The rain
   in Spain stays mainly in the plain'; 'The lower-lying parts of
   the peninsula enjoy most of the precipitation'; 'If you go to the
   mountains, don't expect more than the odd shower.'

4. *Have extra hard evidence in reserve.* Your key points during
   the presentation should have been supported by concrete
   examples, hard data, expert opinion. The Q & A session is a
   good time to dig a bit deeper: 'I hadn't intended to show you
   this, but since you've asked – here is a graph of the results
   our Colombian subsidiary enjoyed when they implemented
   this new system a year ago.'

What if they don't have any questions?

'So, are there any questions?' Silence. I wish I were dead. And the
longer the silence goes on, the harder it becomes for anybody to
produce a question. Two basic techniques to avoid this:

1. *Plant a question in advance.* Before you ever begin, make a
   deal with some ally in the audience that he will ask you a nice
   juicy question at the appropriate time. If, when the time
   comes, several hands shoot up at once, choose somebody other
   than your stooge. And when you do answer your stooge's
   question, don't go on too long about it. It is only an ice-
   breaker; you can expect a supplementary question from a
   'real' source.

2. *Ask yourself a question.*

❑ Any old question to get it rolling: 'A colleague of mine was asking me the other day...'

❑ a 'topical' question: 'I heard some of you in the lobby discussing xyz, and it strikes me that this raises a question...'

❑ an 'urgent' question: 'Your head of human resources came and picked me up at the airport today, so we would have a little time to discuss...'

❑ a 'probing' question: 'I don't think I really did justice to the question of rainfall over the Iberian plateau...'

Very few listeners will even realize that you are answering your own question. Most will be impressed at your competent handling of it.

HANDLING THE QUESTIONS

Making a presentation is a stressful experience at a very basic level ('Why are all these animals looking at me so intently? They must want to kill me and eat me!'), and the adrenaline 'high' can give great energy to the performance. But it is poor preparation for a cosy Q & A forum.

Picture yourself driving at high speed on a country road. The first questioner is like a pedestrian suddenly jumping into the road in front of you, waving his arms.

Your response is all too likely to be abrupt, as you stamp on the brakes: '17.5 per cent, obviously. I thought everybody knew that'; or impatient: 'The answer to that question was on the third graph I showed you.'

You will alienate not only the hapless questioner, but everybody else in the audience.

What this means to you

1. *Change gear* at the beginning of the Q & A session – by changing your position on the platform, or by perching your bottom on the corner of a table. Say: 'Now let's pause for half a minute, while I get my breath back, and you think about what questions you might want to ask me.'

2. Embrace the question. Don't say: 'That's a good question', for fear of the sardonic response: 'That's why I asked it'. Say rather: 'I'm glad you asked that; it gives us a chance to..' or 'That's an interesting angle...'

3. Look keen. Don't :

   ❏ stand with one eyebrow raised ('I can't believe the naiveté of this question!');

   ❏ sigh and turn away ('I'm surrounded by idiots!');

   ❏ interrupt the questioner ('All right! All right! My time is precious!');

   ❏ produce a slick answer ('This is too easy!').

   Much better to:

   ❏ pay close attention, and signal courteous interest;

   ❏ pause, and let them see that you are thinking about the answer.

4. Play back the question to make sure you heard it right. Say: 'Let me re-frame that a little; you seem to be asking...'

5. If the answer has to be a long one, embrace the whole audience. Say: 'We can see, can't we, why Mr Brown has asked this question...'.

6. Check at the end to see if he's happy now: 'Does that answer the question?'

Finish with a bang

If the Q & A session comes at the end of your slot, or just before a coffee break, set up one final question which you can answer with great authority.

Your audience's attention will be at a natural peak, anticipating a change of stimulus, and so you can lodge in their alert minds a strong and positive impression of your competence, and of your main message.

THE INTERNATIONAL ARENA: QUESTIONS AND ANSWERS

When you are working in English (the international business language) with an audience of non-English speakers, you can be straightforward with things like gratitude, praise and enthusiasm.

Working within your own culture, you often rely on sub-verbal signals to transmit these messages. The English, for example, often find it clumsy or embarrassing to say:

> 'You, of course, are an expert audience, well qualified to judge these matters for yourselves. Still, I am grateful for the time you have given me, and really feel that the ideas I will present today can make a big difference.'

Yet this is just the sort of thing that you *should* say, if your audience is listening in English-as-a-foreign-language. They will not feel that you have overstated your point. Rather, they will be happy that you have expressed your positive emotions in a clear and sincere fashion.

The same applies when you are responding to questions. If an Englishman says to an English audience,

> 'That really is a fascinating question, and I am happy to do my best to answer it...'

the audience might groan inwardly. Often it is considered more 'sophisticated' to leave this unsaid – to communicate *by tone of voice* that one is treating the question with great respect.

Your international audience is not so well tuned-in to your tone of voice, or other implicit message channels. Say it loud and clear:

What a useful question! Thank you very much!

PROJECTING YOURSELF

To repeat an idea from the second chapter: your audience will remember only a small part of what they hear, but a great deal of what they see. And a lot of what they see is you.

The way you look, the way you carry yourself, the expression on your face at key moments – these can enhance or destroy your message.

Often it would be wrong to say directly. 'I am a good person and you can depend on me', but you can send the signal loud and clear without speaking a word. In fact, you are doing it most of the time in your social and professional life; if you were transmitting other signals, you would be a flop in both departments. (Think about some of the teenagers you know: clumsy, shy, gauche, graceless, moody, self-centred, erratic, insensitive... and they can deliver all these messages just by the way they sprawl on a sofa.)

Yet we all experience stress when we have an audience staring at us, and that stress affects our body language. (We begin to appear clumsy, self-centred, insensitive, etc.)

Break the vicious circle of stress

Many people get stuck in a loop, just below the level of consciousness:

I'M FEELING NERVOUS

THEY CAN SEE I'M NERVOUS

THEY'RE LAUGHING AT ME/

THEY HATE ME

THAT REALLY MAKES ME NERVOUS

AND THEY CAN SEE IT...

And so the nerves take over the performance.

There are several ways to break the loop:

1. *Make deliberate contact in the first half minute.* Speak a few words personally to one member of the audience, to get a smile and a nod. Then they will cease to appear like a pack of hungry animals, and your adrenaline rush will abate.

2. *Remind yourself that they can't really see your nervousness.* Most of what you are experiencing – the clammy palms, the thundering heart, the blood roaring in your ears – is quite undetectable to the audience. Break the loop by saying, 'They really can't see how nervous I am.'

3. *Remember that the audience is on your side*. They are spending valuable time watching and listening to your presentation. They would much rather see you succeed.

4. *Win a breathing space*. Give them something to look at and think about for half a minute, while you take a few deep breaths and look at them – as people, who are just as nervous about public speaking as you are.

Adopt high status body language

This means:

❏ No hiding – behind lecterns, tables, sheaves of speaking notes, folded arms

❏ Head up, shoulders back

❏ Feet firmly planted, weight equally distributed

Arms relaxed at your sides, ready to move for emphasis and demonstration

❏ Generous, open gestures using the shoulder as well as wrists and elbows

The message you are sending is:

Nothing to hide

What you see is what you get

Nothing up my sleeve

Pleased to meet you

A lot of fidgety behaviour involves touching things, or parts of yourself – fiddling with the pointer, jingling keys in your pocket, scratching your nose, crossing your legs. It provides some kind of psychological reassurance.

If you are prone to this, we offer a suggestion that might help: get in touch with yourself in a way that the audience will not notice. You can try it now:

Make a circle of your thumb and middle finger, leaving the rest of your fingers relaxed. Now let that arm hang loose by your side. Quite unnoticeably, you can press finger and thumb hard together and work out a lot of tension. You can do this on stage from time to time, and nobody will see a thing.

Of course, a lot of fidgeting is unconscious. This is where any good presentations training course will make use of video playbacks. You can arrange the experience – often quite painful, but always fruitful – with a trusted friend, a camcorder, and a rehearsal.

Resist the temptation to try and rebuild your behaviour completely. Your audience will sense it if you try to become someone you are not, and all your efforts to project sincerity will produce the reverse effect: 'Who's he trying to fool?'

Rather, set yourself one target that you can achieve: I will stop tugging at my ear lobe; I will smile more often.

Show, and use, your eyes

The face is a wonderfully complex signalling system, and holds a supremely important position in human life. The mother's face is the baby's first object of study. Most banknotes carry a face: you could get the serial number or the geometrical patterns slightly wrong in your forgery, and survive for a while, but if your George Washington doesn't look like himself, your goose is soon cooked.

Within the face, the eyes are crucial – especially for establishing trust. The poker face of the Mississippi steamboat cardsharp has dead eyes. The guilty man in the dock finds it hard to meet the eyes of his accuser. Nobody ever bought a used car from a salesman in dark glasses.

Meet the eyes of your audience; let them look through the windows of your soul.

In a small group – half-a-dozen people – you can read a lot in your listeners' eyes. If there are more than ten of them, you will not be able to give each individual his ration of eye contact. (Three seconds each, repeated every two minutes, achieves nothing.)

The trick then is to select, say, three people: one towards the left of the hall, one in the middle, and one to the right. Or one in the front row to chat to, one in the back row to project yourself at, one who will smile back at you and make you feel loved and wanted.

Everybody drops his gaze, or stares unfocused into the distance, when he is concentrating hard to retrieve fact from memory, or make calculations.

Exercise

Stare into the eyes of a friend and recite the alphabet – backwards
– without breaking eye contact. Very difficult.

Be conscious of this, and establish a rhythm in your speaking.
During long, taxing 'paragraphs' of your talk, your eyes might
drift to the upper corner of the hall, or out the window. Each time
you reach the end of a 'paragraph', you should deliver the last
idea, or sentence, looking directly into the eyes of one of your chosen recipients.

Then look at what's happening in his eyes: Are you getting
feedback? If you find that he is asleep with his eyes open, that is
valuable information. Time to do something about it.

Take your time

Too much chatter is seen as a sign of nervousness. It is also a sign
that the presenter is overestimating his audience's mental capacity. Slow down.

> We... don't... recommend... that... you... pause... after...
> each... word... That... would... drive... your... audience...
> crazy.
> What we suggest instead... is that you pause... after each
> idea-group... because that's the natural way... for the mind
> of your listener... to absorb what you're saying.

Then allow a much longer pause after you deliver a big idea.
Remember that five seconds will seem like a lifetime to you, on
stage. For your audience, it will be a refreshing oasis of calm, and
they will love it.

THE INTERNATIONAL ARENA: BODY LANGUAGE

❏ In certain cultures, it is inappropriate for a junior to display
high status body language in front of his elders and betters.

If you are going to make a presentation in such an area, find a
friendly local and ask about your standing in the eyes of your
audience. You might have to practise an alert-but-humble pos-
ture.

❏ The American-style smile of confidence is seen in some cultures as insincere – an empty vessel making a lot of noise.

Watch the faces of the locals. Do they smile a lot? When they do, is it sometimes a grin of embarrassment? Observe their politicians and TV presenters.

❏ There are cultures that enjoy touching, and others that don't.

Of course, it is good at times to get closer to your listeners – perhaps by organizing the chairs in an open U-shape, and then patrolling the open space. In places where people expect 'teachers' to maintain a distance, such behaviour might be disturbing.

Synopsis

If you have read this book from start to finish, or if you just run an eye down the contents list, you should feel an underlying structure – beginning with

your audience

then addressing the design of

your message

and only then paying much attention to

yourself.

We firmly believe that this is the best order to work in when you are preparing a presentation.

Start by thinking hard about those who are going to observe your performance. It is they who set the conditions and the limits for your material, and for your behaviour. They play the important role; what happens in the minds and hearts of your listeners is paramount. You serve the audience and support that process.

Your objective should be firm and realistic; your message is the means of reaching that goal. The audience must surely influence your message, at the design stage. If you deliver the same message twice to different audiences, at least one of them has received imperfect service.

Further, when your performance begins, a very early task is to check: Are these people really where you expected them to be? Are their levels of knowledge, their attitudes, their sense of humour all as you predicted? Make space for yourself to read their feedback signals, and modify your performance accordingly.

During a presentation, your mind is working at three levels:

1.   Conscious; requiring attention
2.   Semi-conscious; second nature
3.   Reflex; no effort

An average/immature public speaker, who knows his material well, but is concerned about himself during his performance, is literally *self-conscious*.

The successful, mature speaker is the one who has truly learned to *put his audience first*.

	IMMATURE SPEAKER	MATURE SPEAKER
CONSCIOUS	**ME** 'I'm on stage...'	**MY AUDIENCE** 'Hello...'
SEMI-CONSCIOUS	**MY MESSAGE** 'doing the job...'	**MY MESSAGE** 'for you...'
REFLEX	**MY AUDIENCE** 'anybody there...?'	**ME** 'thanks for listening'

What this means to you

You are already a better-than-average presenter; you want to be excellent.

After every presentation you make, you relive the experience and criticize yourself constructively. Perhaps you ask yourself:

*   Did I handle my slides effectively?

*   Did I cover the material with the right emphases?

*   Did I demonstrate that I am competent?

These are all fine questions. But at this stage of development, it is much better to ask:

*   Did I observe audience reaction during the performance?

*   Did I adjust the presentation according to what I observed?

Afterword

Apart from the OHP and the videobeam, most of what we have covered in this book would be familiar to Aristotle and Macaulay, as well as Abraham Lincoln and Mark Antony (see the appendices).

There is nothing new in any of this; we hope we have provided a useful synthesis.

If you should come up with something completely new in the field of human communication, you will make a mark in the world. Meanwhile, we suggest that you continue to borrow ideas from good speakers wherever you find them.

When you are faced with a choice between the elaborate and the simple, choose the simple. Finally, when all the clutter is stripped away, there are just your audience, your message and you.

A successful presentation makes things happen in the minds of your audience. If you look into their eyes, you can see it happen. It is a great experience.

Appendix 1

Mark Antony's speech

Friends, Romans, countrymen, lend me your ears.
I come to bury Caesar, not to praise him.
The evil that men do lives after them;
The good is oft interrèd with their bones,
So let it be with Caesar. The noble Brutus
Hath told you Caesar was ambitious.
If it were so, it was a grievous fault.
And grievously hath Caesar answered it.
Here, under leave of Brutus, and the rest –
For Brutus is an honourable man,
So are they all, all honourable men –
Come I to speak in Caesar's funeral.
He was my friend, faithful and just to me.
But Brutus says he was ambitious,
And Brutus is an honourable man.
He hath brought many captives home to Rome,
Whose ransoms did the general coffers fill.
Did this in Caesar seem ambitious?
When that the poor have cried, Caesar hath wept.
Ambition should be made of sterner stuff,
Yet Brutus says he was ambitious,
And Brutus is an honourable man.
You all did see that on the Lupercal,
I thrice presented him a kingly crown,
Which he did thrice refuse. Was this ambition?
Yet Brutus says he was ambitious,
And sure he is an honourable man.
I speak not to disprove what Brutus spoke,
But here I am, to speak what I do know.
You all did love him once, not without cause;
What cause withholds you then to mourn for him?
O judgment, thou art fled to brutish beasts,
And men have lost their reason!
Bear with me,
My heart is in the coffin there with Caesar,
And I must pause, till it come back to me.

The plebeians talk among themselves, agreeing with all Mark Antony's points so far. Recovering from his fit of stage grief, Antony then teases the audience with Caesar's will:

> Which, pardon me, I do not mean to read...

> You are not wood, you are not stones, but men;
> And being men, hearing the will of Caesar,
> It will inflame you, it will make you mad.

One more side-swipe at the conspirators:

> I fear I wrong the honourable men
> Whose daggers have stabbed Caesar;

Antony comes down from the podium, and makes his audience form a circle around him and Caesar's corpse:

> If you have tears, prepare to shed them now.
> You all do know this mantle. I remember
> The first time ever Caesar put it on.
> 'Twas on a summer's evening in his tent,
> That day he overcame the Nervii.
> Look, in this place ran Cassius' dagger through.
> See what a rent the envious Casca made.
> Through this, the well-belovèd Brutus stabbed,
> And, as he plucked his cursèd steel away,
> Mark how the blood of Caesar followed it...

> This was the most unkindest cut of all.

The mob starts howling for revenge.

Good friends, sweet friends, let me not stir you up
To such a sudden flood of mutiny...

> I come not, friends, to steal away your hearts.
> I am no orator, as Brutus is.
> But, as you know me all, a plain blunt man
> That love my friend...

> ... I only speak right on.
> I tell you that which you yourselves do know,
> Show you sweet Caesar's wounds, poor, poor dumb mouths,
> And bid them speak for me. But were I Brutus,
> And Brutus Antony, there were an Antony
> Would ruffle up your spirits, and put a tongue
> In every wound of Caesar, that should move
> The stones of Rome to rise and mutiny.

> *All:* We'll mutiny.

Finally, Antony pulls them back from the brink to read out to them Caesar's will, bequeathing to the people all Caesar's walks, arbours and orchards for their pleasure.

Then he turns the mob loose to run riot.

Appendix 2

THE GETTYSBURG ADDRESS

Four score and seven years ago our fathers brought forth on this continent a new nation, conceived in liberty, and dedicated to the proposition that all men are created equal.

Now we are engaged in a great civil war, testing whether that nation or any nation so conceived and so dedicated can long endure. We are met on a great battle-field of that war. We have come to dedicate a portion of that field, as a final resting place for those who here gave their lives that that nation might live. It is altogether fitting and proper that we should do this.

But, in a larger sense, we cannot dedicate – we cannot consecrate – we cannot hallow – this ground. The brave men, living and dead, who struggled here, have consecrated it, far above our poor power to add or detract. The world will little note, nor long remember what we say here but it can never forget what they did here. It is for us the living, rather, to be dedicated here to the unfinished work which they who fought here have thus far so nobly advanced. It is rather for us to be here dedicated to the great task remaining before us – that from these honoured dead we take increased devotion to that cause for which they gave the last full measure of devotion – that we here highly resolve that these dead shall not have died in vain – that this nation, under God, shall have a new birth of freedom – and that government of the people, by the people, for the people, shall not perish from the earth.

Abraham Lincoln

Delivered at the dedication of the cemetery at Gettysburg,
19 November 1863